War Time Memories

*A Collection of 'real life' stories
from those who fought during
and lived through World War II*

•

Compiled by Michael Bentinck

ISBN 0 9526157 4 6

Published by
Michael Bentinck
Bentinck Books,
10 Henry Morris Road,
Impington, Cambridge, CB4 9YG.

Printed By
Fieldfare Publications, Cambridge, UK

Typeset in New Baskerville, 11pt

Contents

                                                    Page

Introduction..v

Foreword..vi

Acknowledgement..viii

Chapter I - Arthur Seager's Story........................1

Chapter II - Geoffrey Wilson's Story.................20

Chapter III - Ruth Lindner's Story....................46

Chapter IV - Walter Adams's Story....................77

Chapter V - Constance Ronan's Story.................81

Chapter VI - Alice Stokes's Story.......................86

Chapter VII - Moses Luff's Story.......................95

Chapter VIII - Bernard Carr's Story.................100

Chapter IX - Joanne Walker's Story.................110

Chapter X - Joan Walton's Story.....................119

Chapter XI - Mr D G Malyon's Story.................124

Chapter XII - Andrea Hoyland's Story..............127

Chapter XIII - Edith Smith's Story....................131

Chapter XIV - Anthony Dixon's Story..............136

Letters & Poems..140

End Note...152

Introduction

The book you are about to read is full of true stories, taken from the war time memories of people from all walks of life, that gave and suffered so much for our lives today. I know just how lucky I am that these good people trust me and allow me to be the one to write up their true stories. In order that others can read about what living through a World War was like for them.

You will read of what it was like to be a young navigator in the R.A.F., flying in those big bombers called Flying Fortresses and about the dangers that went hand in hand with such a task; of one brave man's endeavours to evade capture from the Japanese and of how the nightmare of those days were to stay with him, in his mind, for the rest of his life; what it was like to be a rent collector in war torn London, as well as the dangers, you will read of all the amusing things that this job entailed; the true stories of a Nurse, a Land Army Girl, a soldier in the Home Guard and an Evacuee. We will also hear about one young lady who entertained the good people of war-torn Sheffield with her singing and dancing, which was bravely done with the rest of her troop, while the bombs rained down.

I hope that you will find your journey through this book an enjoyable one and that it will be of great interest to you.

Michael Bentinck

Foreword

By Stanley Chown M.B.E. F.C. F.A. C.G.

It is a great honour and privilege for me to be asked to write the foreword to this wonderful book, of people's war time memories. I, like so many of my generation, have many memories of life through two world wars. In World War One I was just a young child, when my father marched off with his young comrades to fight for King and country, so that we could all remain free. When he finally returned home, he spent the next three years in hospital because he had been badly wounded, in thirteen places. Thankfully, he survived to tell the tale and he became a wonderful, loving father to my brother and I. So when World War Two started, I think it fair to say, that I had a good idea of what lay ahead of me, as I went off to fight for King and Country.

I have always said that Michael Bentinck has a God given gift for writing the true stories of what ordinary people gave and suffered in World War Two. I know that many of you will have read my own true story in Michael's book *A Will To Live* and of course, I can't thank Michael enough for the wonderful way he wrote my heartfelt story.

I will never forget the days that Michael and I sat together as he wrote down my story and of the many memories that it brought flooding back to me. Now once again Michael has visited many more brave people and in his own heartfelt style, has written down their memories of those never forgotten times in their lives. In *War Time Memories* you will read the true stories of people from all walks of life that answered the call to serve their Country. I say thank you to God, that they found Michael, so that others can read of the part they played in marking the paths of history and for giving us our today. I really am one of the lucky ones. For now that I am 90 years old, I look around me at our world today and I thank God for the wonderful life that I and my darling wife, Dora, have shared together. We have a life time of memories to share, but we will never forget our own 'War Time Memories'.

S. Chown

Acknowledgement

My thanks go to the wonderful people who have allowed me to write and share their war time memories with you my readers. Once again I have made many more friends as, thankfully, those that I have written about have become good friends to me and my wife Hilary.

I thank my dear late father, so very much, for not taking his story to the grave with him. Although it was very upsetting at the time he shared his story with me, in those last three months of his life, I now know what a privilege he allowed me. He will always be 'my dad, my hero' and I thank him so much for changing my life for the better.

To all the people that I have met around our great country, when I have given my talks on World War Two, I say a big thank you to you all, for your very kind words after my talks. To all of you that have written to me, to say how much you have enjoyed all my books, I thank you for taking the time to write. I would like to thank my dear friend Stanley Chown, M.B.E., for writing the foreword to this book and for the friendship that he and his dear wife, Dora, have shown to my wife, Hilary and I. They have shared with us so many memories, of their journey through life together.

My heartfelt thanks go to two very special people in my life, for all their help and support: my dear friend and editor, Keith Dixon, who works so hard behind the scenes to make sure that my writing is ready for publication, along with all the other help and advice that he gives me and thanks also to my lovely wife, Hilary, for the love, help and encouragement that she gives me every day.

I would also like to thank Fieldfare Publications, my printers, for all the help and guidance that they have given in the production of this book.

Last, but not least, I would like to thank you, my readers, for supporting me by helping my chosen charities.

Best wishes,

Michael Bentinck

Chapter I

Arthur Seager's Story

Arthur's story was sent to me by his proud wife, Barbara and daughter, Carol, shortly after his death, on February 6th 2001. Arthur put pen to paper for this story in the mid eighties. He gave the story the title 'The Will To Win' and when you read the story you will understand why. Arthur went on to write many hymns and poems, one of which I am privileged to publish in this book.

I will leave you, my friends, to read on - but I hope that this story and the poems that Arthur wrote are a tribute and a lasting memorial to him.

At the capitulation of Singapore I was a Corporal in The Royal Norfolk Regiment guarding the harbour. It was about mid-day and the Officer in charge of the Guard instructed us to lay down our arms and await the arrival of the Japanese, who were expected for the unconditional surrender later in the day. I discussed with the men of my section what the surrender would mean to us and we decided unanimously to attempt an escape. We searched all over the abandoned naval base and found that all the launches and pleasure craft had been damaged beyond repair by the Royal Navy, the only craft available was an old abandoned sampan which was partially submerged in the mud of the outgoing tide. Wading up to our knees in mud and slime we managed to refloat the sampan, but we could only manage to find one good complete oar and the blade of another that had about two feet of shaft. Rations had been scarce for the past few days and so all we could muster were a few packets of biscuits. We did managed to fill two, four gallon, petrol cans with drinking water. We also found a Tommy Gun, a Lewis Gun without a stand and about two boxes of ammunition.

By the time I and the other six men had managed to squeeze into the sampan along with the weight of the guns and ammunition, it was no more than six inches above the water. Our intention was to make for the open sea and take a chance of being picked up by the Royal Navy. However, on rowing out into the harbour, we were hailed by a group of men in a small boat tied up to a large Chinese Junk, which looked somewhat like an old galleon. We paddled over to them and discovered that they were men from the Malayan Royal Artillery. The three man crew of the Junk tried their best to prevent us from boarding, but we forced our way on board and with signs we made them understand that we wanted them to sail us to Australia and if they didn't take us we would work the Junk ourselves and they would have to come with us.

It was not possible to allow them to go ashore as they may have been pro-Japanese, as so many of the Malays were at that time. They discussed our ultimatum with excited voices and much gesticulation, none of which we understood. The oldest member of the crew, a small wizened man, then fetched a bowl of water and two rice serving dishes, then sitting crossed legged on the deck he floated the rice dishes in the bowl of water. He smashed the two dishes together and then raised his arms above his head and shouted "BOOM", tears were running down his cheeks. We all understood that he was trying to tell us that the harbour was very heavily mined and that he didn't know a way through the minefield. We held another conference and decided to go on. Now it was getting dark and the tide was running in. To get the Junk out of the harbour it was essential to have a high tide.

Not a sound could be heard from Singapore and we were silhouetted against a wall of flames. The town was ablaze from end to end. We assisted the crew to turn the big windlass, raise the huge mainsail and then the anchor. The creak of the ropes and blocks along with the rattle of the anchor chain echoed across the harbour and took what seemed an eternity. Any minute we expected to be fired upon from the shore, or see a patrol boat sent by the Japs to investigate. We sighed with relief when the operation of setting up the Junk was complete and thanked God that there was a breeze to fill the mainsail.

It was not long before we were out of the harbour and gliding into the inky darkness. It seemed strange to glide along without the throb of an engine. The only sound being the swish of water and the creak of the mainsail. The little old man was standing on deck giving orders to the man at the helm which was operated by a system of block and tackle. At times he crouched over a very old compass with a lighted match cupped in his hands, but for most of the time he plotted his course by the stars.

I had, some time before, decided that if we did strike a mine I would not be injured, but blown to pieces, so I settled down in the bow of the boat so that I could see the mine that would kill me if we did strike. Everyone was tense, I don't believe a word was spoken for about three hours, when suddenly the little old man danced around the deck, laughing and shaking hands with everyone. We knew then that we were clear of the minefield. The crew could now relax and they took turns to go down to the cabin for a smoke of opium, which they prepared by rolling the opium into a small pill before placing this in the bowl of a small metal pipe with a long stem, the bowl was heated over a small oil lamp, they then inhaled the fumes given off. We were all dead tired but dared not all go to sleep at the same time. The crew could still be a possible danger and we were still concerned about the Jap patrol boats.

Another hour must have passed when we caught sight of another boat on our port bow, about a hundred yards ahead and heading towards us. We woke all the men and grabbing guns and ammunition, we tripped over each other in the excitement to line the port side. Not a sound could be heard or a light seen from this boat and as it came on towards us it looked like a big expensive pleasure cruiser. As we got nearer there was still no sign of life on board. We held our fire as it came nearer and nearer. I'm sure every man thought as I did, that whoever was on board had decided to surprise us by running alongside and boarding our Junk. It came alongside as we expected, grazing our port bow and then a steel hook caught in our mainsail and brought it down with a crash to the deck. We waited, still holding our fire and hardly daring to breath, the seconds ticked by into minutes. The sweat was pouring down our faces as we waited for the fusillade of fire that never came. All the time we were taking stock of this ghost ship which sailed in from the darkness and suddenly we realised it was indeed a ghost ship. The steel hooks they were using to board us were from the ropes of the empty lifeboat davits, the curved arms of these were swinging out at least two feet from the side of ship. Undoubtedly this had been an evacuation ship that had been caught by the Japs and abandoned by those on board. Together we all rose to our feet and cut the ropes that held the two boats together, the ghost ship glided off into the darkness as silently as it had come.

Of course we might well have found food on board and we could certainly have done with it, but I'm certain that not a man on board would have stepped onto it to look. What a relief we felt when it finally disappeared from view.

We now had the job of repairing the rigging of the mainsail, this took the crew at least another two hours, but luckily our jib sail still kept us moving, even if it was only at a crawl.

I made myself comfortable on the deck, determined not to fall asleep, but the next thing I knew I was opening my eyes in bright sunshine and we had stopped moving. I jumped to my feet and found we were at anchor, about two hundred yards away from the shore, just off one of the many small islands off Singapore. We thought this was a trap and that there must be Japs on the Island but we never found out. The intention of the little old man was that we should leave his ship and trust in providence to be picked up from this island by a friendly ship before the Japs found us. He told us to camouflage ourselves with large straw hats, black baggy cotton coolie trousers and tunics. This would allow seven or eight of us to be on deck at the same time without causing any suspicion should we be spotted from the shore. We thought that this was a crazy idea and that we were going to be shot at from the shore at any time. As it turned out we didn't have to refuse his suggestion this time, the Japs put an end to it for us.

We suddenly heard Jap dive bombers in search of an easy target. One suddenly swooped down from the sky straight at us. The three Malays immediately dived overboard and swam as fast as they could for the shore. It must have looked quite a natural scene to the Jap pilot, especially as the Junk was at anchor and we were standing on deck in native dress, so he veered off without firing a shot. Two men, against our advice, jumped into the sampan in an attempt to fetch them back. At the end of the day they still hadn't returned, which meant now our only means of getting ashore was to swim. We were about to up anchor and sail the Junk ourselves, when a small boat came from around the other side of the island. The boat turned out to hold nine Australian soldiers, one of which was badly injured and a lieutenant. They had been cut off in Malaya and were fired upon from the shore when escaping. The wounded soldier had been hit by shrapnel in the back. We pulled them on board, set sail and decided that with these men on board we would now definitely head for Australia.

Just because we now had an officer aboard we didn't intend to be given orders, especially as it was our Junk. We were giving him a lift. We all discussed this and decided to work on a majority vote, the officer would have a casting vote if necessary. He was asked to organise the shifts for the smooth running of the ship and to take charge of all the rations and water on board. This consisted of about five tins of bully beef, a few packets of biscuits and at least two tons of rice, as well as two barrels of dirty drinking water alive with mosquito larva.

Things ran smoothly for the following two or three days but with very little wind we made very slow progress. We grew sick of rice boiled in sea water, we had to conserve the fresh water for drinking. During the afternoon of the fourth day we came within sight of the black coastline of Sumatra.

As far as the eye could see, there was an unbroken line of jungle and mangrove swamp right down to the waters edge. It looked inhospitable. That evening the wind dropped altogether. We should not have sailed in so close, the sails slapped against the mast and we drifted in on the tide. Every few minutes the hull scrapped on the coral reefs beneath. We had no alternative but to drop anchor and wait for a breeze.

We lay at anchor all night and in the morning found we were aground with quite a list on the deck. During the day we spotted a dugout canoe being paddled towards us through the mangrove swamp by a very tough looking pygmy. He wouldn't come very near but we eventually persuaded him with offers of presents to come closer. By means of hand signals we managed to convey to him that we would swop a bag of rice for some fish. He paddled off and was soon back with about a dozen fresh fish. We lowered down a sack of rice to the canoe, almost sinking it and he paddled off looking very pleased with himself for having made the best bargain of his life.

We did not realise that this was the start of the monsoon season and by the following morning quite a stiff breeze was blowing and the tide was in. We all cheered and hoisted the sail and with the aid of poles managed to free ourselves from the reef. We then raised the anchor and were away. The wind increased to gale force and the sea became very rough so we hoisted every inch of sail. The Junk sliced through the sea like a racing yacht. It was a thrill after being sat at anchor for so long to feel the deck vibrate under our feet. It was not long before we realised we were taking on water, a plank must have been sprung when we went aground. Luckily the Junk was fitted with a very old hand pump and by continuous pumping we found that we could hold the level of the water. That evening the gale increased and so did our speed. It was a pleasant feeling to be putting distance between us and the Japs, or so we thought. Suddenly with a tremendous rending sound the mainmast snapped and thirty feet of timber tangled with sail came crashing down to the deck. It was chaos for a few minutes. Luckily the Jib was still standing and it managed to keep us moving, be it at a very sluggish pace. No one was injured, so after untangling the mess and taking stock of our position, we decided that our only chance now was to follow the coast until we came to a river big enough to take our Junk and deep enough to allow us in close to the bank so that we could cut down a suitable tree to replace the mast. The storm also took the boat that the Australians had come aboard with, which was another blow to our spirits.

Using the Jib we managed to reach the Tambi river and a small village at the mouth ruled by a Chinese trader. He knew of an organised escape route down the Indragiri river to Padang, some two or three hundred miles away on the west coast. He promised to help us and said he would use his men to cut down a tree for a mast, but it didn't happen and when asked why it wasn't done he always replied "Tomorrow a mast will come". As a consolation we had all the tropical fruits you could name, the deck was piled high with them, but we would have given anything for a crust of bread.

The days passed by and we became very unsettled as we knew we were a sitting target for the Japs. We were now worn out from having very little sleep, suffering from dysentery and fever. The Chinese trader was an expert at striking a bargain and after days of "Tomorrow a mast will come", we were prepared to swim to Australia. The trader's offer now was that we should give him our Junk, seeing that it was useless in its present state and he would take us in his motor launch back along the coast to the mouth of the Indragiri river, the first stage of the escape route. He must have been aware that the escape route had closed down days or weeks before our arrival. We eventually agreed to his scheme and were packed into the launch like sardines. We travelled all night and were soaked to the skin due to the pouring rain. We arrived at a small village and spent the following day resting. The local population didn't want anything to do with us. At night they lit huge bonfires, keeping on the smoke side of the fires to protect themselves from the huge mosquitoes, which settled so thickly on the skin, that when I brushed them off my arms they left a brown stain.

The native's favourite pastime seemed to be catching crickets. They scorched the wings off on the hot embers and ate them with great relish. The Chinese trader had now left us, having kept his part of the bargain. After many days of heart breaking slog across Sumatra, by river, through jungle, swamp and mosquitoes, we eventually arrived in Padang in a very bad state of health. Thank God we didn't know that worse was to come.

At Padang we were told by the Dutch military to hand over our arms as we were going to be evacuated by a Royal Navy submarine. The Dutch were intending to offer no resistance to the Japs, in the hope that they would be allowed to have their freedom, just as the Vichy French had. By keeping us in Padang the Dutch had a good present to hand over to the Japs. All the

Dutch boats were guarded by the Dutch army, so it was impossible to make a second escape, even if we had the strength. A submarine had arrived and been used a few days previously to evacuate soldiers and the Dutch told us that it was coming back. Unfortunately time ran out for us and early one afternoon we were informed by the Dutch that the Japs were about to march in and they would offer no resistance.

The Japs came in with fixed bayonets and machine guns. We were lined up wondering if it would be a bayonet or bullet. After a pep talk by a Jap officer we were held as prisoners in the Dutch barracks. One could understand the Dutch position. Many of them had wives and children living in Pedang and if they could show that they were co-operating they may have been able to retain their freedom.

After a few months of working on airstrips and blasting walls we were in a poor state of health. Food consisted of a small quantity of rice and a green swamp weed. On the 9th May 1942 we moved camp to the port of Belawin Deli, near Medan, arriving on May 12th, having had a very uncomfortable journey. On the 15th May we embarked on a small steamer, the 'England Maru'. Accommodation was in the hold. Shelves had been built four feet apart which was just enough space to lie flat. The latrines were wooden boxes with a hole in the bottom and hung over the side. With the men having dysentery and sea sickness conditions were terrible and the only way to the latrines was by walking over bodies, causing a lot of cursing. Rice was cooked on deck by the Japs. They tipped a large quantity of rice into a wooden vat and then placed a steam hose into the middle of the rice.

Our biggest fear was being torpedoed by the allies. We knew that if we were on board we would not have a hope of getting out. On the 25th May, after ten days on this hell ship, we arrived at Mergui, Malaya.

We disembarked and marched to Mergui school in pouring rain. There was not enough accommodation for all of us and when we were joined by another thousand Australians, who arrived from Singapore, many of the men had no cover at all. By now, along with many others, I was suffering from dysentery and malaria. Many men had already died from these diseases or malnutrition.

We were put to work at Mergui and this consisted of enlarging the airstrip. With only the clothes that I stood up in, I soon learned to leave clothing behind in camp when I went off to work, so that I could wear something dry at night. Day after day it rained, rain so heavy it made your skin wrinkle as if you had soaked in a bath all day. It was possible to hear the storms coming many minutes before they reached us.

During early August 1942 we were once again on the move, this time in two small ships which had open holds. There wasn't sufficient space available for us all to sit down. The Japs soon made extra space by beating everyone within reach, making us sit up with our legs apart, so that another Prisoner of War (POW) could sit between our legs. In the early hours of the second day we arrived at the mouth of the Tavoy river, we climbed aboard barges and went on to Tavoy. We then marched the four miles to camp. When leaving Mergui we were known as the 'British Battalion', under the command of Captain Apthorpe, of the Royal Norfolk Regiment. Captain Apthorpe was a well loved officer. He stood up for us and as a result endured many beatings.

Once again we were sent out on work parties, enlarging the airfield. By this time, twenty two POW's had already died. Twenty two was also the average age of the dead.

It was at Tavoy that Sergeant L. Bullock, Royal Air Force, at great risk to himself, managed to obtain wireless parts and he was able to construct a receiver which continued to operate right through to the end of the war.

On the 21st of October we were once again on the move. This time we went by barge to the river mouth and then changed onto two small ships arriving at Moulmein the following day.

It was at Moulmein that I contracted diphtheria. I reported sick to the Australian Medical Officer, Lieutenant Colonel Coates. I was placed in quarantine in a disused bamboo and attap hut which had a mud floor. All I possessed was a straw mat and one thin blanket. Food and water was brought to the door. Colonel Coates explained that he had no drugs with which to treat me. However, later in the day he arrived with a small bottle which contained about one ounce of yellow liquid called flavine. I took a small sip and rolled this to the back of my throat, holding it as long as possible before swallowing.

After about ten days I was out working again and I realised that I was starting to lose all the feeling in my hands and feet. I was also starting to suffer from double vision. This caused me to step up or down at the wrong time which often caused me to fall or stub my toes. Things got a lot worse later. I was eating some grains of rice when some came down my nose, choking me, it left me speaking with a nasal tone, as if I had a cleft palate. I still suffer from this choking once or twice a week and it usually finishes up with a sneezing fit. I again reported sick and was told to eat pap. Pap is rice boiled to a thin gruel. The M.O. explained that the double vision and loss of feeling was caused by being forced to work so soon after diphtheria and had now caused polyneuritis.

At the time that I was sick, most of the camp had been moved out to Thanbyuzayat, Burma, to start work on the death railway. My health did not improve. The numbness was creeping up my legs. About three weeks later the remaining sick were moved out on foot through jungle paths, en-route to Thanbyuzayat, a distance of about thirty miles. After about fifteen miles, we stopped and spent the night in an open clearing. I was in a terrible state by this time, running a fever. I didn't want anything to eat but I was very thirsty. If it were not for my good friends I wouldn't be here today. I just fell to the ground exhausted, all I wanted to do was to be left alone. Fortunately my friends informed the M.O. that I was unable to stand. It was also fortunate that we had reached a railway track at the side of a clearing. No trains were running because a bridge somewhere along the line had been destroyed by the RAF sometime earlier. However the Japs had a hand pushed truck and they had loaded all their baggage into it. My fear was that, seeing that I couldn't walk, the Japs would finish me off. The Japs must have been in a good mood, as the Commanding Officer talked them into putting me on top of their baggage.

The Jap guards sat on a bench seat at the front of the truck which was pushed along by four Burmese men. When the truck reached a decline the men jumped onto a foot rail and rode down the slope. My fellow POW's had left earlier, following the railway track to Thanbyuzayat. After about an hour we caught up with them walking along beside the track.

Suddenly the men were shouting at the Japs on the truck that the bridge was down. They were grabbing at the baggage on the truck trying to slow it down. I could see myself going over the edge of the bridge. Knowing that the Japs were unable to understand English, I had to act quickly. The truck was still travelling at five or six miles an hour and I had no strength to climb down and I couldn't jump. Fortunately I was sitting facing the back of the truck, so I just toppled off in a sitting position, landing on my hands and knees. I thought I had broken my wrists and smashed my kneecaps, as the pain was terrible. The baggage was reloaded and I was pushed back on top of it and our journey continued.

We had been going for about an hour when the Japs started shouting; I turned my head to see a huge swarm of wild killer bees spiralling towards us. They attacked everything that moved, the air was black with them. The Jap guards left the truck and ran into the jungle, leaving me perched high on the back of the truck not able to move. I was soon being stung on my hands, head and face. I had no strength left to climb down so, for the second time that day, I leaned forward and toppled off and to save further damage to my hands and knees, I landed on my shoulder.

I was unable to stand and as I was the only target left, the bees followed me down. It's surprising what passes through your mind at times like these. I thought, "this is it. After all the suffering. What a way to die. After all I've been through, to be beaten by a swarm of bees." I didn't know what to do. Brushing them off wouldn't help, even if I had the strength. I crawled on elbows and knees into the edge of the jungle with the bees swarming on the back of my neck and my head. And then suddenly I had an idea. I must kill them! I buried my face into the ground to protect my eyes and with sloth like movements reached round to the back of my neck, grabbing a handful of bees and squeezing them to pulp. I then repeated this performance for what seemed an eternity as my movements were so slow. At last all the bees seemed to be dead and I was alive. Although I had received hundreds of stings I don't remember feeling any pain. I now became worried that I had been left behind by the Japs, so I crawled back as fast as I could. The Japs were just coming out of the jungle, laughing with each other and rubbing their stings. They re-loaded the baggage which had fallen off the truck and once again pushed me back on top. We then set off again down the track. We eventually came to the end of the line, which was where the bridge had been blown up at a river crossing. A train carrying steel was waiting on the other side of the river waiting to transport us to Thanbyuzayat. The walking POW's had already arrived at the river crossing and were being loaded onto barges to make the crossing. I was feeling very ill by this time and I was almost unconscious. A good friend to everyone, Chief Petty Officer Tucker carried me to the barge and from the barge to the railway trucks.

I don't remember much about the rail journey, other than I was burning up with fever and that it was dark when we arrived. I was carried into the bamboo hospital hut and made as comfortable as possible by one of the orderlies. No special bedding, just my straw mat and thin blanket.

The Medical Officer for the hospital hut was an Australian called Major Fisher. He examined me and gave me a shot of precious morphine. I can remember him telling the other patients to keep quiet as it was unlikely that I would last the night. It would have been so easy to die, to get out of the pain and suffering like so many others had done. They would say "I can't go on" and they would be dead by the next day. If I could only have made contact with my family at home, to let them know how ill I was, I would have been able to die in peace. Because I was unable to do that, I had to live, I had to carry on, so as not to let them down. I also had to keep awake if I wanted to live, because I knew that if I fell asleep I would not wake up. It was a great attraction.

The following morning the orderly came with tweezers and pulled hundreds of stings from my head and the back of my neck. Major Fisher came later and asked lots of questions, which as I was unable to speak, I answered with shakes and nods of the head. I gradually recovered and found that I could walk if I kept my legs very straight, if my knees bent I would collapse on the ground, unfortunately this happened very often.

The hospital wards were full of men with dysentery, malaria and ulcers as well as all the amputation cases. These amputations were performed by lieutenant Colonel Coates, who after the war was Knighted by the Queen. A local anaesthetic, made up of cocaine and various plants from the jungle, was administered. Often the amputations were carried out in the open because of the danger of dust from the atap roof. I have seen the patient smoking and carrying on a conversation with Lieutenant Colonel Coates as he was sawing through the bone.

The hospital food was very poor, because the Japs considered that as the non-working sick were not using any energy working, they only needed half the food of a working POW. Certain numbers of POW's were required each day for working parties. If these numbers were not reached, owing to the large number of sick, the Japs just raised the temperature at which a Malaria patient could be excused work, say from 102 to 103 or 104 degrees. The Medical Officer had to carry out these instructions as the Japs had threatened to make all of the sick men return to work.

The death rate in camps varied from ten percent in Burma to thirty percent in Siam. A young POW thinking about his own death wrote the following verses. His lines expresses how many at the time felt:

> *What shall I think when I am called to die?*
> *Shall I not find too soon my life has ended?*
> *The years, too quickly, have hastened by;*
> *with so little done of all that I intended.*

> *There were so many things I'd meant to try,*
> *So many contests I had hoped to win;*
> *And Lo, the end approaches just as I*
> *was thinking of preparing to begin.*

I gradually recovered from the polyneuritis and as advised, to help the double vision, I boiled grass and drank the liquid. If I was fortunate enough to obtain an egg I would save the shell

13

and crunch a small piece between my teeth as I, perhaps wrongly, believed this would increase the calcium in my body.

Skin diseases were rife in all the camps and I in my turn, suffered from them all - scabies, eczema, ringworm etc. The treatment for these was a thick, liquid, mixture of quicklime and sulphur. You could smell the burning and feel the pain, but it worked.

Before we left Thanbyuzayat the camp was bombed by four American liberators causing many deaths and injuries. As if we hadn't enough to put up with. They returned the following day and bombed again. The camp was in the centre of a rail yard with Jap barracks near-by. The Japs had large red crosses on their barrack roofs, which is why we received the bombs. The Japanese did not abide by the rules of the Geneva Convention.

I was soon moved to the Eighteen kilo camp. It was here that Private Pagani escaped and found his way to a British officer in Burma. The Officer had stayed behind in Burma to organise resistance with the Christian Karen tribe. Private Pagani was the only man ever to escape from the Japanese and live. The British Officer, Major H.P Seagrim, a Norfolk man, gave himself up to the Japs after they carried out their threat to execute one Karen tribesman for every day that he was free. A monument has been erected in the form of a village sign at Whissonsett, Norfolk, in memory of his self sacrifice. Private Pagani was awarded the Military Medal and Major Seagrim the Victoria Cross.

To the reader it may seem that some of the diseases we suffered from were not very dangerous, but they should remember that the environment we lived in had a great effect on our health and lack of recovery.

No one in their wildest dreams could imagine the nightmare conditions we lived in. Teeth were extracted without anaesthetic, an infected ingrowing toenail was removed by cutting straight down the centre of the nail and pulling off the two halves.

We eventually moved from camp to camp working on the railway from Burma to Siam. Over one hundred and forty men had now died from our group. A friend of mine could recite Kipling's poem 'If' from memory and he would recite this in the dark when we were resting. The words of this poem fitted our situation exactly.

If
by Rudyard Kipling

If you can keep your head when all about you
Are losing theirs and blaming it on you;
If you can trust yourself when all men doubt you,
But make allowance for their doubting too:
If you can wait and not be tired by waiting,
Or, being lied about, don't deal in lies,
Or being hated don't give way to hating,
And yet don't look too good, nor talk too wise;

If you can dream- and not make dreams your master;
If you can think- and not make thoughts your aim,
If you can meet with Triumph and Disaster
And treat those two impostors just the same:.
If you can bear to hear the truth you've spoken
Twisted by knaves to make a trap for fools,
Or watch the things you gave your life to, broken,
And stoop and build'em up with worn-out tools;

If you can make one heap of all your winnings
And risk it on one turn of pitch-and-toss,
And lose and start again at your beginnings,
And never breathe a word about your loss:
If you can force your heart and nerve and sinew
To serve your turn long after they are gone,
And so hold on when there is nothing in you
Except the Will which says to them: "Hold on!"

If you can talk with crowds and keep your virtue,
Or walk with Kings-nor lose the common touch,
If neither foes nor loving friends can hurt you,
If all men count with you, but none too much:
If you can fill the unforgiving minute
With sixty seconds' worth of distance run,
Yours is the Earth and everything that's in it,
And - which is more - you'll be a Man, my son!

The railway was now finished and in April 1944 we were moved by road and rail to Saigon, French Indo China. The accommodation was timber built barracks, close by the docks. We had running water and electric light. The quantity of rice improved due to the fact that we were in a rice growing area. Work was either on the docks, on the airfield or in oil storage plant.

On December 24th 1944, Christmas Eve, four of our men had been seen by the Japs running away from the Jap clothing store. They were spotted running into our hut. Unable to catch the men, the Japs made three searches of our hut without finding anything. During the early hours, we were called out to parade in open order and called to attention. We were informed that we would stay to attention until the guilty men owned up. Jap guards with fixed bayonets walked up and down the open ranks, watching for the slightest blink. The sick were also carried out on stretchers. We stood to attention from the early hours, until late afternoon. We were burnt by the sun and bitten by flies during the day and we were cold and bitten by mosquito's at night. Captain Apthorpe walked through the ranks giving encouragement with an odd glance here and there. He was very proud of us because we all knew who the guilty men were, but we were not prepared to inform on fellow service men. The men responsible were given away by a Dutch-Javanese soldier from another hut. The guilty men were arrested and hung by their wrists so that their toes were just touching the ground. A funnel was forced into their mouths and they were filled with water. They were then beaten on their extended stomachs with a baseball bat.

On January 12th 1945 we had the first air raid. One hundred and forty dive bombers attacked and surprised the Japs. The bombers must have been aware of our camp as this time not one bomb landed on us. Ships were sunk and over one hundred planes were destroyed on the airfield. The Japs now became very touchy and nervous. They instigated a roll call every hour of the day and night. This became very tiring after a hard day's work.

The end came suddenly with the dropping of the atom bomb. Then leaflets, dropped by the Royal Air Force, informed the local population of Saigon that their friends, the French, would be returning. They hated the idea that the French colonial power would once again be returning to run their country. The crafty Japs had given them their independence a few months earlier and installed a puppet government.

Various factions were now fighting each other and there was a risk that they would attack us. We asked for arms to protect ourselves but we were advised against it. A British naval officer, dropped by parachute with a jeep, informed us that the best thing he could do was make the Japs responsible for our safety. It was like living with a time bomb. Freedom was so close yet so far away.

This was now the start of the Vietnam war and I believe it could have been avoided if the Americans or British had taken over French Indo China. It seems that General De-Gaul insisted on the French returning.

I returned by air to Rangoon, then by ship home to Southampton, England. During my life as a POW I had travelled through five countries: Malaya, Sumatra, Burma, Siam and Indo-China.

I have not told this story to anyone before now, it would have been too painful, but writing it down is like thinking aloud in an empty room. It was so easy to die under those conditions. It took 100% effort just to keep alive. I was determined that I was not going to die in a prison camp. I know that it was not physical strength that kept us alive but more a state of mind. It was fatal to live in the present and think about what was happening to you. You had to live in the past or look to the future. You focused your mind and energy on getting home and no more. I was the only one of the six men who escaped on the Junk to survive and return home.

After three and a half years of being away we received many shocks on returning to England; the faces you expected to see were no longer there. Some married men returned to find that their wives, assuming that they were dead, had remarried. There were no psychiatrists or counsellors to offer advise to us. No one seemed to care. The day peace was declared, caring seemed to end. All through the war people cared for each other, but this seemed to end with the end of the war.

On my return to England I joined a Territorial Army Unit, started in my small country town. It was so hard to meet parents and friends of old comrades to be asked "Have you any knowledge of my son or my husband?". In time I learnt to avoid these situations as the answer would so often bring tears.

I was twenty four years old and I remember that I often looked back and thought of the suffering and pain that I and many others, endured. It is unbelievable to think that all this had happened to me and that I had made it home again.

To understand how we returning POW's felt, I can do no better than to quote the words of Ernest Gordon, from his book 'RIVER KWAI'

> *'It is not surprising that we were moody, restless and irritable, we felt that at any moment we might be seized and deprived of our freedom. The Japanese were still with us; they entered our dreams. If we dreamed of the day's events in our new environment the guards would be there, walking unnoticed among the people in the street. If we strolled past with a friend they'd reach out and grab us. If we dreamed of open fields or rolling moors our old hosts would be there, advancing, closing in on us from every side. No matter how hard we tried to flee they would always catch us.'*

Those men that had returned hungered for each others company and for the comradeship we once shared. Our friends must have had the impression that our imprisonment was one huge, rollicking party. We fought off a great loneliness, a loneliness that was increased by the fact that so many of our friends had not returned. Old familiar spots were haunted with their faces. Whenever we met with other former POW's we loved to talk of the brilliant plans we had made and of the great things we were now going to do. We were convinced that we had learned lessons important to mankind and we were going to implement them. We thought we had come home to a world at peace; instead we found a world already preparing for the next war. Having had as much reason to hate as anybody, we had overcome hatred. Yet we returned to a world divided by hatred. Communists hated Capitalists; Capitalists hated Communists; Arab hated Jew; Jew hated Arab; The labour force hated Management; Management hated the labour force; Politicians hated Politicians.

A moral cynicism was sapping the strength of society. Half lies were not only condoned but regarded as smart. There were many who had remained un-touched by the welter of the holocaust. What had happened on the battlefields, in mass bombings, in concentration camps, the blood, pain, suffering, heart-break and death remained totally beyond their comprehension. They did not share in the hopes and agonies of mankind; they had no sense of involvement, they had no part in the universal fellowship of those who bear the mark of pain.

Ever so brightly and ever so meanly they prostrated themselves before the almighty dollar and the trembling pound. We encountered some who were actually sorry to see the war come to an end, because they had such a good time and had done so well financially. Nations had survived the war, but few people asked, what for?

•

When Arthur's will was read it was found that he had written this hymn for his own funeral and he asked that it be sung to the tune of St Clements in memory of him. It is an honour to have it in my book as a lasting tribute to Arthur.

SONG OF DAVID
by Arthur Seager

I lay me down beside still waters
Where our dear Lord did lead me to
Through Death's dark vale to fresh green pastures
He raised me head to see anew

No fear had I with Thee beside me
Thy Rod and Staff did comfort bring
O'er rocky paths, through darkest valleys
I raised my voice your praise to sing

A table there was laid before me
My enemies were all in view
To see my head with oil anointed
My soul restored to start anew

The home that now within I dwell
The Son of God does hold the key
Goodness and Mercy you will find there
Come enter within and stay with me

Chapter II

Geoffrey Wilson's Story

The following story was sent to me by Mrs Mary Wilson, of Cranfield, Bedfordshire. I had the privilege to meet Mary when I gave my talk 'War Time Women' to the Cranfield Women's Institute. I mentioned at the end of my talk how important it was for everyone to write down their memories of their journey through life, to leave for their families to read after they have gone. A couple of weeks later I received from Mary, notes that her late husband, Geoffrey, had written relating to his memories of his days in World War Two, as a Navigator in the R.A.F. As you read on you will discover that Geoffrey was in bombers, those big flying fortresses of World War Two. We owe so much to the boys of the R.A.F. for the part they played in giving us our today, for most of us know how much we owe them for the part they all played in the 'Battle of Britain' in 1940. Many of us have seen films like the great classic 'The Dam Busters'. We can only imagine the fear that the bomber crews must have felt on those raids, especially "The tail end charlie" - the rear gunner. It is my privilege to feature Geoffrey Wilson's story in this book, as my tribute to what he and all his brave comrades, gave for our today.

Supply dropping in support of S.O.E. operations in Northern Europe 1944-1945

During the German occupation of Europe, an active underground resistance movement operated throughout the continent, conducting sabotage and intelligence operations against this occupying power. The movement was supplied largely by sea and air and the technique of aerial supply is the subject of the following account.

The aircraft used were, in the main, Halifaxes and Stirlings, flown by 38 Group. R.A.F. Lancasters were occasionally used but not to any extent. The Halifaxes were the aircraft of which I have personal experience, so I will confine myself to details of operations in these aircraft.

They were general purpose aircraft which could readily be used for the dropping of paratroops and for the towing of military gliders, both of which were 38 Group activities. The troops were dropped from a hatch in the floor at the rear end of the fuselage and to allow adequate room for them all to be carried, the mid upper turret was removed from these aircraft. The rear turret being the only armament, apart from a vickers gas operated gun sighted in the nose and fired by the bomb aimer.

For supply dropping operations, the supplies were carried in cylindrical containers, each fitted with a parachute stowed in one end and attached by a static line to the aircraft fuselage. The cylinders were fitted into the bomb bays, with 12 in the fuselage and four in each wing bay, as far as I can remember. Additional supplies were carried in large baskets carried forward of the paratroop hatch in the fuselage and similarly supplied with parachutes attached by static lines to the inside of the fuselage. The containers were attached by means of a lug-to-hook in each bomb bay position and held rigid by means of adjustable clamps at front and rear. The hook could be released by means of an electro-magnetic mechanism actuated by the bomb aimer. Each container was individually connected to a switch in the bomb aimers compartment, these switches were set out in banks of 4 or 5 with a common switch controlling each. There was a master switch that had to be thrown before any release of the containers could take place. A timing device, similar in principle and speed to a telephone dial, was connected and this could be preset so that the containers could be released either in batches of 4 or 5 singly in line behind the aircraft, or simultaneously if necessary. All of these devices could be tested out on the ground prior to take off, provided the master switch was not thrown. This, of course, did not prevent the odd bomb aimer forgetting and consequently depositing the whole load out onto the runway occasionally. The loads could vary and experiments were made to carry a jeep and a light gun, three parachutes being on the jeep and two on the gun. This together with petrol supplies in the wing bays and about four troops in the fuselage, would constitute a small reconnaissance force capable of being dropped far behind the enemy lines.

The crew consisted of 6 members: the Pilot, Navigator, Bomb-aimer, Wireless Operator, Flight Engineer and Rear Gunner. The pilot flew the aircraft and was also, irrespective of rank, the captain of the aircraft. He made the decisions depending on his own observations and information fed to him by the other crew members.

The navigator was responsible for getting the aircraft to the rendezvous and home again and for ensuring adequate height to clear the highest ground en route. He was also responsible for keeping an estimated time of arrival, an accurate log of the journey and noting anything of interest supplied by other crew members. The navigator was totally enclosed in his position and could not see outside, so anything noticed by the crew would be passed to him via the intercom for him to note in the log. He had access to radio aids and direction finding equipment, of which more details follow later.

The bomb-aimer was responsible for dropping the supplies on receipt of signals from the ground. His was the primary responsibility of navigating the aircraft between the rendezvous and the dropping point - he had to watch for pin-points to accurately position the aircraft. He was also the second pilot, for it took two men to both lift off and land these aircraft. While the pilot flew the aircraft off and back onto the runway, the bomb-aimer would attend to the lifting and lowering of the undercarriage, the positioning of the flaps and locking of the throttles etc. Radio silence was observed on these trips but the wireless operator had to maintain a listening watch at regular intervals on stated frequencies to collect information such as weather reports. He would recall instructions and diversions, in the case of bad weather conditions back at base, which would make it unsuitable for landing. He was also equipped with a direction finding aerial and could obtain bearings on radio beacons for use by the navigator.

The flight engineer had his own instrument panel at the rear of the pilot's seat and kept a log of fuel consumption, engine temperatures, etc. He pumped the fuel between the fuel tanks to keep the aircraft evenly loaded and generally assisted the pilot to keep track of the aircraft's performance.

The rear gunner kept an eye out for enemy planes and was usually the first to shout "Bandits at 12. o'clock". He also reported back anything he saw which might be useful to the navigator. He took bearings to assist with navigation and he was able to check the containers as they left the aircraft in case of a foul up in the bomb bay, which did happen sometimes. His was a very lonely and cold job, as he was so remote from the rest of the crew, who were clustered together in the nose of the aircraft. It was the rear gunner that was most likely to be hit in the event of an attack by enemy fighters, as they would come up behind the aircraft and shoot as they overflew the slower moving bomber. These rear gunners were very brave, special men and I was privileged to fly with them.

All crew members were supplied with Mae Wests, an inflatable life jacket. These the crew wore all the time in case the aircraft came down in the sea, the aircraft also carried an inflatable dinghy in the wing. Parachutes were also carried but these were stowed in accessible positions to be clipped onto a harness worn by the men in the event of an emergency. Escape boots were also worn, these were ordinary knee length flying boots but if it was necessary to bale out, the top of the boot could be cut off with a pen knife, supplied for this purpose, when they became to all intents and purposes indistinguishable from ordinary shoes. A small first aid kit was carried by each man containing among other things, morphia and needles to be used in the case of severe injury. A small pack of iron rations and cloth maps were issued to be used if lost in enemy territory. It was also usual for each crew member to carry a .38 revolver whilst on operational flights.

The bases from which these activities were conducted, were in the main in Wiltshire and Dorset. Netheravon was the most famous but there were others. Tarrant Rushton was the one at which I was based, which was about 12 miles from Bournemouth, you can imagine the hardships. This was due in the first instance, I imagine, to the nearness to France, which was the country most concerned in these supply drops early in the war. The aircraft there had a short radius of action and needed to be based within easy reach of their dropping zones.

Later on, four engined aircraft with an extended radius of action, made this of less importance but these aircraft were used for glider towing and for paratroop dropping. The proximity of these bases to Salisbury Plain, which was a large military base, again made these airfields easily accessible for training of airborne forces on the plain. It did however, add appreciably to the length of operation necessary to reach Northern Europe and Scandinavia and it is with operations in these countries which I myself was chiefly concerned.

Crews would be called over the tannoy system at approximately midday for a briefing at 2pm. This was held in the briefing room, which was a large nissen type hut approximately 60ft by 30ft containing forms, tables and a platform at the front much like a stage. The crews would assemble and each crew would sit together, the various members having the necessary maps and charts with them. They would be given details of the night's operations by the various experts such as the Meteorologist.

The Met officer would be the first speaker and he would give details of the weather situations over Europe in much the same way as the television reporters report the weather on television today. Of course nobody had a television in those days, so it was all very new for us at that time. Apart from the general situation, certain items were of great importance to aircrews and these were dealt with in great detail. The first of these was the barometric pressure both at base and over the dropping zone. The aircraft altimeter was adjusted to read height from barometric pressure and it was essential that it be accurately set. These operations were conducted at a height of 600 ft, above the sea and about the same height over land, depending on the height of the land above sea level, so that a variation of 100 ft could mean the difference between hitting an obstacle like an electric pylon and flying over it. The low altitude was essential to avoid being picked up by enemy radar but it was necessary when dropping to climb to 1000 feet to allow the parachutes time to open, so that the load could be dropped slowly and not be smashed to pieces on the ground. The altitude at which the temperature was below freezing was also something to be noted.

If the rendezvous point happened to be a lake, it would look like a black pool in the snow from above but if the surface was frozen, then the snow would fall on the ground and surface of the water as well and the lake would be indistinguishable from the air. There was also the question of ice forming on the wings of the aircraft, which would be hazardous as well as possibly putting out of action some of the aircraft instruments, e.g. the air speed indicator. Wind direction and speed had to be known, also visibility and height of cloud etc. All this would have been collected from reconnaissance pilots who had flown out during the preceding period, as well as by radio information from the continent.

The navigation leader would then give details of heights to be flown and tracks, for points of entry over the coast. He would give details of any known hazards, anti aircraft batteries etc. He would have details of any enemy coastal beacons which were available to take bearings on and would give details of rendezvous points and dropping zones, radar frequencies, etc.

The bombing leader would give details of loads to be carried and method of dropping height for the drop. This was followed by a radio expert who would give details to the wireless operators of frequencies to be used, plus call signs and times of listening watch. He would also give the 'Colour of the day', that is the colour of a Very cartridge which would be fired off in the event of the aircraft being challenged by either a friendly fighter, or naval forces. This cartridge could be fired from a Very pistol, stowed next to the pilot and the colour was changed every 4 hours. A failure to fire the correct colour could of course, have serious consequences.

The intelligence officer would have the latest information from the field. He would give the codes expected to be flashed from the ground, the position of the dropping zones and the expected time of arrival. Any other relevant information would also be given at this time.

Finally there would be a short talk from the Squadron Commander on generalities and then the pilots would leave to inspect the aircraft, followed by the gunner who would check his guns. Then the wireless operator and flight engineer would go to their respective specialist sections, leaving the navigator and bomb aimer, to spend the rest of the afternoon drawing in tracks and working out courses and speeds and deciding a take off time to achieve the desired ETA (estimated time of arrival). This would take up until tea time, when after tea in the mess, crews would assemble again for a final briefing, in case the weather or conditions at the receiving end had altered and then out by truck to the aircraft.

It would then be time for take off and the bomb aimer would occupy the second pilot's seat and the crew would be clustered behind a bullet proof bulkhead at the rear of the pilot. These seats, being provided between the wing spans, were considered the safest places in the event of a crash on take off. The pilot would already have been given a chit giving his initial courses and on becoming airborne would turn to this course whilst the rest of the crew settled down in their respective positions. The navigator was placed just in rear of the bomb aimer in the nose and he sat sideways to the line of flight so that he could easily contact either the bomb aimer, or the wireless operator without using the intercom. The intercom system was not all that efficient in these aircraft and it was better to pass courses and speeds etc by means of chits so that there was no mistake in transmission.

Runs to Scandinavia from these bases, invariably seemed to route out over the Wash and this was a good place to pin-point a definite point of departure as something like four rivers flowed into the Wash and it was easy to ascertain the exact ground position of the aircraft. From base to this point the bomb aimer would be reading off ground positions while the navigator would be checking on radar. An initial wind speed and directions would have been found and any necessary alteration of course made. After crossing the coastline the bomb aimer could not obtain further pin-points and the trip would continue entirely on radar.

The radar equipment was known as 'Gee' because it was invented by a man called Gee. I don't know any more about him but this is how the system worked: there were a number of Gee chains, each covering a different area of Britain and its approaches and later extended on to the continent but this description is of a typical chain. The chain consisted of a master station and two slave stations set at the points of a triangle, say with 80 to 100 mile sides. The master station would transmit a signal which would radiate out in all directions like the ripples when a stone is thrown into a pond. Upon hitting an aircraft radar aerial, the signal would cause a blip to appear on the radar screen inside the aircraft. At the same time the master station would trigger off a second signal from the first slave station which similarly would radiate in all directions and hit the aircraft radar aerial. Due to the variation in distance which the two signals had to travel, there would be a lag in the time at which the slave signal hit the aircraft and this lag could be seen and measured on the aircraft radar screen. The measuring device was incorporated electronically in the radar tube and was made visible by the throwing of a switch. Similarly this could be repeated for signals between the master station and slave station two and all signals could be locked in position and measured on the radar screen. Charts were carried on which curves had been printed. These curves joined all points on the surface of the chart in which the time lag of the radar signals was of a fixed value e.g. 5.1 5.2 5.3 etc. By marking the intersection of the appropriate two curves, a position could be ascertained and transferred in latitude and longitude to the navigation chart. A fix taken every 10 minutes would keep an adequate check on positions and if there was any appreciable drift away from the desired track, a new course could be worked out and a fresh ETA calculated. It was not, of course, possible to stop the aircraft, so the alteration would be worked out for a time 6 minutes in advance and alteration made at that time.

All this was very fine and straight forward but a system designed for bomber raids carried out at 10,000 to 25,000 feet could not be expected to function free from interference at 600 feet. The interference was known to navigators as 'Grass' because it looked like grass and seemed to grow like grass. At first small shoots appeared at the base of the screen and these grew as the distance from base increased, until the screen was covered with waving stalks and no signals could be seen at all. So other methods had to be used and this involved the cooperation of the rear gunner and a device known as a flame float.

A flame float consisted of a small cylinder, the dimensions of which I forget but it could be held in the hand. It contained a firing pin, a small explosive charge and a supply of phosphorus powder. The cylinder could be thrown out of the aircraft and on hitting the surface of the sea, the device collapsed and the firing pin exploded the charge and scattered the phosphorus powder onto the surface of the sea, where it burned with a blue flame for a period of 2 to 3 minutes. This would be done by the rear gunner whose turret was equipped with a scale. This scale registered the direction port or starboard in degrees, in which his guns were pointing relative to the fore and aft axis of the aircraft. He would then train his guns on the point of flame and could read off on his scale the amount of drift which the aircraft was making. This could then be compared with the calculated drift and any slight alteration made to maintain the correct track. In the event of a large alteration due to a change of weather conditions, e.g. passing through a thunderstorm, a 60 degree change of course could be flown for 6 minutes, followed by a 120 degree change in the opposite direction for 6 minutes and a final change of 60 degrees back to the original course would form an equilateral triangle. A drift could be taken on each course and a new wind velocity and direction computed on a small computer that was supplied for this purpose. The ETA in this case would have to be extended by 6 minutes. By these methods, a landfall could be made with 5 miles either side of the intended point.

In theory it is possible to fly into Europe over any point on the coastline but in practice this is not the case. If you are intending to find a man flashing a torch in a field, then it is essential to know accurately, the point at which you enter the continent and to be sure that you are in that position. To quote two extreme cases, the southern coastline of Norway is a mass of inlets and islands and it is impossible in the dark to be absolutely sure of the exact position of the aircraft. The west coast of Denmark is exactly opposite to this, an absolutely straight North, South, coastline which may be crossed anywhere without any distinguishing feature to give an absolute position. The aim therefore was to head for some distinguishing feature that could easily be identified and in the case of South Norway, the port of Kristiansand was the ideal place. A port with harbour installations and industrial features. Kristiansand could easily be picked out and serve as a turning point onto the new course into the interior. Similarly on the straight coast line of Denmark, there is a gap where the sea flows into an island lake and this gap also made a very good entry point. The Germans were equally aware of these facts and took good care to place heavy anti aircraft batteries at all these points, so that it was like going into the wrong end of a firework display. This served as a further confirmation that the point of entry was the correct one.

It was not a very practical idea to fly direct to the field or similar open space designated as the dropping zone, or DZ. The aim was first of all to find some features easily distinguishable in the dark, a lake or railway junction, perhaps a small town or junction of two rivers. This was known as the rendezvous, or RV. With the information on wind speed and direction, obtained during the sea crossing, it was possible to set a course that would take the aircraft within a reasonable radius of the RV. The overland section was not all that long, it would take only half an hour or so, even in these big slow aircraft, to get well into the centre of Denmark and the bomb aimer would be looking out during this period for any points he could identify. The snag arose if the RV did not appear at the appropriate time. Here there was a conflict of opinions. The navigation leader back at base would have insisted that the dead reckoning navigation plot be kept up throughout the trip but the Squadron Commander would advise "stooging around for a while" to try and locate the DZ. Once the pilot indulged in this "stooging" around, all the navigator's hard work throughout the trip went for nothing and there would be a great deal of nail biting and harsh words muttered, with the intercom switched off. However for the purpose of this narrative, we will assume that all is well and we have found the RV without difficulty. The DZ would be perhaps 20 to 30 miles from the RV and a course height to fly and airspeed would have been worked out in advance by the navigator. The pilot would turn onto this course over the RV and head for the DZ. From now on the aircraft was under the control of the bomb aimer, who would be flat on his stomach watching for any distinguishing land marks down on the ground. The navigator meanwhile would be counting off in half minutes, the time down to the ETA at the dropping zone and giving any information about features that would be seen below the aircraft. At ETA the navigator would give the pilot the word and whether the DZ had been identified or not, the pilot would commence a 360 degree turn which would take him round and back over the same spot again. The degree of turn would depend on the type of country, with wide turns in flat country and steep turns in the mountain areas. Assuming that the ground party were on site, the second run over the dropping zone would bring a response from the ground, a torch would be flashed giving the code agreed upon.

Upon making contact, the navigator, flight engineer and wireless operator would move to the rear of the aircraft and open the paratroop hatch in the floor of the fuselage. Above this hatch were two lights, one red and one green and the bomb aimer would switch on the red one as a 'stand by'. The ground party meanwhile would lay out three lamps in a straight line, running in the direction of the prevailing wind, the torch being flashed at the 'downwind' lamp. The navigator as he passed the pilot would hand over a chit giving the course to fly out and the safe height to clear any high ground on this course. The pilot would then turn, under the direction of the bomb aimer, onto a course taking the aircraft directly over and in line with the three lights, the height and air speed having been previously agreed. As the aircraft passed over the first light, the bomb aimer, would release the load simultaneously flashing the green light in the fuselage. On receiving a 'green' the three crew members would get their shoulders behind the baskets and heave them out through the paratroop hatch, the rear gunner at this point counting the parachutes passing below his turret to ensure that all had safely left the aircraft. On the words "Containers away" the pilot would immediately turn onto the course to steer out and at full throttle climb to the safe height. This made it difficult for the crew members in the fuselage to regain their seats but at this stage in the operation, it was a question of getting away and on the way home as quickly as possible. The theory behind the drop was that the containers would leave the aircraft over the leading light and be carried by their own velocity, forward of the row of lights. When the parachute opened, the wind blowing down the row, would drift the package back, so that they fell between the first and last lights. We had found, when acting as reception parties on practice drops in the UK, that this is in fact was what happened and the ground party did not have to go very far to retrieve the containers. The aim then was to head for the coast as quickly as possible and then to set course for home.

In theory the navigation back was as painstaking as that on the outward trip but in practice one usually set an approximate course and waited for Gee signals to become readable, when an accurate position could be found and a course for base worked out. The navigator was really the only one who concentrated at all in this part of the trip. The rest of the lads took their coffee and snacks, at this time. The trip back was always long and tiresome and it was a job for the crew, especially the rear gunner, to remain alert. 'Wakey Wakey' tablets were issued for crews to take if they found the tendency to doze off too great to resist. A radar beacon was kept on at base and it was possible to home on to this. On landing the crew immediately went to a de-briefing session, where they were asked questions about the trip to try and obtain as much information as possible about the journey, while it was still fresh in the minds of the crew. After this a large meal, which we were really too tired to eat and then to bed. This then constituted an S.O.E., supply dropping trip, but there are other items which do deserve a mention, such as the Rebecca Eureka Direction Finding System.

This was a homing device which could be worked from a motor car battery, quite a technical achievement for those days and one which could allow the underground workers its use without arousing the suspicions of the occupying troops. The ground equipment (Eureka) was housed in a small box with a short aerial attached. The airborne equipment consisted of a radar set with a radar tube calibrated vertically and three aerials, one under the nose end and two in the wing of the aircraft either side of the fuselage (Rebecca). The nose aerial transmitted signals to the ground and the Eureka set converted the frequency and retransmitted the signals to the aircraft. The change of frequency was necessary to avoid waves being returned from trees and buildings and giving a wrong position. If the aircraft were pointing directly at the Eureka aerial, then signals of identical strength would hit both receiving aerials in the wings but should the aircraft be turned away to one side of the ground aerial, the aerial away from the signal, being partially screened by the aircraft nose, would receive a weaker signal. The aim therefore was to turn the aircraft into the stronger signal until both were of equal strength, then the aircraft would be heading direct for the ground beacon. The received signal appeared on the tube in the shape of a bat's wing and it was known as this to the navigators. It travelled along the surface of the tube, from top to bottom, as the aircraft approached the ground beacon and the tube was calibrated in miles distant from the beacon. As the aircraft approached, the scale could be switched, say from 25 miles full travel down the tube to 10 miles and by this means it was possible to position the aircraft directly above the beacon with some accuracy. The importance of this device in S.O.E. work was that if there was no response from the ground over the dropping zone, it was possible to home in on one of these beacons and drop the load at a permanently staffed base hidden in the country, where the equipment could be assembled at leisure and distributed as required by the underground movement. We did not have to do this ourselves in practice the beacons showed up quite well over Denmark, where there were no mountains to interfere with reception but in Norway, the mountainous country prevented clear cut signals from being received. However, in Denmark, the people on the ground were always very efficient and loads were dropped on the designated dropping zone.

Much of this work remains secret and probably the true state of affairs will never be known in my lifetime. I can only go on what I have read and studied myself in library books. Rumours have been circulated via the newspapers that one of the underground teams in France was taken over early in the war by the Germans and this was not known for some years later, so all supplies and personnel were dropped straight into the hands of the enemy. I did not do drops in France and cannot comment any more on this. We had our doubts about Denmark, because the reports were always of efficient drops but I have since read a book called "Two Eggs on my Plate" written by a Danish member of the underground movement, which shows that these people were indeed very well organised and that the supplies were used for the purposes intended. As regards Norway we were, due to our experience, given the job of flying troops to Oslo, to take over the country the day after the war finished. This was accomplished by the rather novel method of flying the Flying Control Officer over to Guardermoen airport, the nearest one to Oslo and dropping him on the runway on the end of a parachute. There he took over the flying control and brought the rest of the aircraft in safely. On landing we found that our troops were really not needed. The drome was under the control of the underground movement, their chief had taken over the German C.O's car and the place was alive with Norwegians wearing armbands and all very well armed. This could not have been organised overnight, so we must assume that there was a very good underground movement and that our supplies were once again put to good use.

Was it frightening? The quick and honest answer is yes it was, we were all scared stiff but this needs to be qualified. These specialist units were all very remote from the rest of the war effort and we only came into contact with other air crews doing the same jobs as we were and dropping paratroops. When you are all doing the same thing and taking the same risks, it is more acceptable than if you were completely on your own.

On mention of the squadrons leave - it was easy to come by and fairly frequent but once on the airfield, there were no weekends away. Every day was a working day and life consisted of flying activities in one form or another. I did not appreciate either the difficulties or the worry of the job until years after when the Suez crisis came upon us. This was another airborne operation and had it grown into a full scale war, it would have certainly meant a recall to service for me and for thousands of people that were my age to return to airborne activities. Having married and had a family by that time, I would not have wanted to undertake the same risks again. So it really took me a full decade to find out the true nature of the job that I and my comrades had undertaken in World War Two.

It has taken me another 25 years to decide that it might be worth writing it all down to leave as a legacy to others to know of the part, I and my comrades played for their today, for these are just some of my War Time Memories.

Squadron:	298 Airborne.
Pilot:	R.F.Ashton. (Bob)
Navigator:	G. Wilson.
Bomb Aimer:	F. Olver. (Freddie)
Wireless Operator:	Charlie. A. Coleman. (Jock)
Flight Engineer:	D. Atkins. (Derek)
Our Brave Rear Gunner:	H.J. Piper. (Harold)

•

Dear Reader,

When Mary first sent me Geoffrey's notes she explained to me, in an accompanying letter, that they were both from Sheffield, or as she wrote in her letter 'Sheffielders'. Having done my War Time Memories programme with BBC Radio Sheffields presenter, Rony Robinson, I feel sure that his listeners will enjoy reading one of their fellow Sheffielder's stories. I would also like to share with you one of Mary's memories that she shared with me in her letter and I quote.

"Several years after the war, Geoffrey and I took a holiday in Norway, a wonderful country but still at that time the people had a great deal of hatred of the Germans. I'm quite sure we should have felt the same way had we been occupied. At one part of our travels through Norway we stayed in a little town, come village, at the end of a Fjord and Geoffrey was able to talk to the proprietor of the small hotel where we were staying. His English was quite good and he said that during the war he had kept hold of his car but of course he had no petrol on which to run it. The battery of his car was used to light up the lights for the R.A.F. to

drop their supplies. As you can imagine this part came at the end of his story but I know that he and Geoffrey sat long into the night sharing their memories of that time in their lives. After this he could not do enough for us and took us on fishing trips and tours up into the mountains. We had a lovely holiday with such happy memories, we always intended to go back but sadly we never made it."

I hope that like me, you found Geoffrey's notes of great interest. I feel sure that any R.A.F. personnel reading it will understand the technical details much better than us mere mortals can. It has been a privilege for me to write up Geoffrey's notes, for that's the only part I have played in bringing this story to you. The credit must all go to Geoffrey and as I said at the start, it is to honour his memory and that of his dear comrades that I am pleased to feature it here. I must also thank his dear wife, Mary, for it was she that was kind enough to send me Geoffrey's notes. She also sent me another true story that happened in Geoffrey's life, before she knew him. When you read it you will see why I told her how brave I thought she was, to allow me to write it up here but as she said, it was part of Geoffrey's life before she knew him. See what you think to the following true story.

This is a tale of true love, travel and politics but if you are expecting a sensuous story of high jinks under the blankets you will be sadly disappointed, for this is the most chaste love story ever written, for reasons which will become clear as the tale progresses. It is not even a very happy adventure, for some grief and suffering comes into it but it has the supreme virtue of being true. I can vouch for this personally as all these adventures happened to me and a girl.

It all started in the winter of 1943 in the great Canadian port of Montreal, in a temperature of something below freezing. The streets were piled with snow which did not melt but stayed deeply rutted where the tracks were kept clear to allow the street cars to run. The St. Lawrence river was completely frozen and great ice flows piled up against the Montreal bridges. Montreal, being mainly French Canadian, was like a western hemisphere Paris, it was full of cafes and restaurants, exotic food, no licensing hours, night clubs open until the early hours, a far cry from the drab towns of my native Yorkshire. The French really understand the art of good living and into this centre of glamour and excitement we were sent to enjoy a weeks leave, after having successfully completed a navigation course at St. Johns, 20 miles outside the city. I had previously taken a bombing and gunnery course in Ontario and was anticipating a return to the U.K. to complete operational training and eventual operations in Europe. All of this was for the future and at the time all the navigators were looking forward to a few days of pleasant relaxation after the concentrated activity of navigational training in the cold temperatures of the Quebec winter. We moved into rooms in one of the many bed and breakfast houses which had sprung up in Montreal and reported to a central depot each day to see whether we were on a UK draft and then, that being our only obligation, we were out on the town for the rest of the day. The place was packed with air crew in transit: British sailors, taking over tank landing craft to be used in the eventual invasion of Europe; various Merchant Navy seamen, who were there in peacetime as well and a fair number of U.S. servicemen, en route for England or the Pacific theatre. For Montreal was a staging post for trans-shipment to all the various theatres of war. Every place of entertainment was full to overflowing and nowhere more so than the R.A.F. club, where we eventually made our way. There were R.A.F. clubs in all the large towns in Canada and in England, mainly staffed by local volunteers, where meals and facilities for letter writing, dancing or just lounging about were available.

I was sitting in the lounge of the club when I looked up from the magazine that I was leafing through and there stood the most attractive girl that I had ever seen. She was small, dark and vivacious. She had large dark eyes and masses of wavy black hair, so dark that it shone, mere words cannot do justice to her beauty. If, however you have seen the film 'West Side Story' you will have seen her twin, for she had the looks of the heroine of that film, as well as the accent. She was indeed as I was to discover, Spanish speaking, a native of Mexico City, one Virgilia Steck Camacho, the only daughter of a doctor of that city but with several brothers. When we had talked a little she said, you will always remember my name as it is the same as that of the President of Mexico.

I have, it is true, always remembered her name but not because it was the same as that of the Mexican President! What was she doing 3,000 miles from her home in Montreal, all on her own? Here we must pause and turn to the political side of the story.

Before World War II there was no such organisation as the United Nations. There was however, a League of Nations, a similar organisation dedicated to the prevention of a further world conflict. In this it was manifestly unsuccessful. However, it was rather more successful in other fields. The eradication of the breeding grounds of the locusts was one project and we now no longer hear of the plagues of locusts which once ravished Africa. When World War II came along, the League of Nations was looked upon as a failed organisation and little more was heard of it. Some sort of organisation was kept in being for part of the League of Nations was the International Labour Office which dealt with labour relations across international borders and when I had managed to coax Virgilia out to an all night restaurant for coffee, she told me she was a translator of ILA. I had previously congratulated her on her command of English and learned that she was fluent in five or six languages. She had also translated at conferences held in the United States and Canada but she did not enlarge on this. It didn't take much deduction to realise that this was a semi-secret organisation, the personnel of which would, if we lost the war, melt away but if we won would be expanded into what we now know as the United Nations and this of course happened.

So, many dates followed and we spent a delightful week sampling the night life of Montreal. She had a small flat in the town so I was able to find her easily but of course we were not circumspect. The Spanish race are very jealous of their girls' reputations and the slightest breath of scandal would have meant her rapid return to Mexico, a neutral country and she wanted to be where the action was. So did I, although I altered my ideas a little when I became operational and had to face up to the flak over Europe but at this time we were a couple of idealists working for a better world and we were careful to keep to the cafes and clubs where we could be seen and I never did get to see her flat.

This idyllic existence lasted for a week when I received an order to join a draft and travel to Eastern Canada (New Brunswick) as they were short of a navigator. Virgilia came to see me off at Montreal railway station. She had taken an hour off work and came dressed in a black astrakhan coat with a brilliant red lining, fur boots and a small black hat like an Egyptian fez but with a silver chain clasp which fastened on the coat, such glamour and at a time when the English girls were not even able to obtain stockings. This was to be the last time we were to meet but not by any means the end of the affair as you will see as the story continues.

I travelled to Moncton, New Brunswick, by train, a 30 hour journey skirting the banks of the St Lawrence river and eventually shipped out from Halifax, Nova Scotia, to England. At this point in the war, the bomber offensive over Germany was still being actively pursued but the demand was for airborne fleets to be created to transport the paratroops and tow the gliders, which would be required for the invasion of Europe. So I found myself drafted into a training programme for airborne work and eventually crewed up and trained for Halifax Bombers. Airborne invasions are few and far between and in any case those which were proposed were largely cancelled because the ground force's advance was so rapid. The bread and butter operations of these Squadrons was the supplying of the underground movements which proliferated through out Europe and we were chiefly concerned with supply drops on northern Europe. I have covered this in my other notes and as this is not a technical write up, I will pass over this part of my career, suffice to say that as we were getting into the swing of it all, the war came to an end and I only completed about half the tour.

During this period Virgilia and I corresponded, I writing to the cover address in Montreal and she to my home address in Sheffield, where my parents forwarded the letters on to the unit at which I happened to be. Marvellous letters, the Spanish races are much concerned with matters of the heart and I can recall such phrases as - although we are separated by these great oceans and continents, my heart is with you all the time that you are flying. Perhaps a little trite now but when you are living in a Nissan hut in wet and cold conditions with perhaps a few casualties and yes there were always casualties, then these words were a great morale booster. Once the war in Europe finished we were all pleased and anxious to celebrate, not least because we had lived to see the end of it and these celebrations, lasted about 12 hours for me.

Now I must divert for a time to the field of strategy. Hitler had always said that if he fell he would bring all of Europe down in ruins with him and we had no reason to believe he would not carry out this threat. So the Allied armies made haste to consolidate their victory and place troops in strategic positions to prevent action by Nazi units, to sabotage essential locations in Europe.

This was comparatively easy as the armies were already in force over on the continent. There was one country where it was not easy to place troops quickly. This was Norway, access to which was only possible by sea, which took time. It was therefore decided to despatch an airborne force with all speed to Oslo, to hold the country until seaborne forces could be brought in. We, being experienced in this type of operation, were therefore instructed to fly with the troops to Oslo, with all speed. We took on board about 10 paratroops with supplies in containers in the wings and a jeep lashed under the aircraft. This was done on all the Squadron aircraft and constituted a sizable mobile force as we set off from base to Oslo. The weather was fine and we were flying in daylight so it was a good trip. Unfortunately, on the first trip we had low cloud over Oslo and were forced to return to Scotland but eventually landed on the second day, unloaded the troops and supplies and returned to base. Now the problem with airborne operations is always re-supply. A man can only take what he can carry on the end of a parachute and you cannot drop stores at the time of the drop because the packages will hit the troops on the way down and casualties will be high. Although we landed with the troops on this occasion, we still adopted the same techniques as in wartime and so we were obliged to make further flights to bring in petrol, food and other items to keep the force supplied. Eventually we did 5 trips to Oslo and settled in to a regular routine: up at 2am; breakfast and the briefing; airborne at dawn; into Oslo by 11am; return to base by 5pm; dinner; bed.

Our mail was placed in pigeon holes in the mess so that we could collect our letters at breakfast and on going into the mess one morning, I saw that a letter had arrived from Virgilia. Up until this time we had been under strict instructions to empty our pockets before going on an operation, so that no evidence of our personal affairs, or the locality of our base, would be available to the Germans, in the event of our being forced down and captured. As the war was now over I saw no harm in putting the envelope in my battledress pocket, so that I could read it later.

Soon after breakfast we were off once more to Norway and on reaching the airport, Gardemoen, whilst waiting for take off to return to base, I opened the letter. Virgilia had written to say that she would shortly be setting out for Europe. A conference had been arranged to be held at the palace of Versailles. The Prime Minister, Churchill, Marshall Stalin and President Truman, would also be there together with their attendant advisers and a team of translators, one of which would be virgilia Comacho. This would take place in July 1945 and since they would be based in Paris, it was implied, though not stated, that I would make an effort to be there. So there I was on this airfield which only a couple of days before had been enemy territory with all this top secret information in my possession and wondering what I was going to do about it.

I must now digress again to say that this conference did not take place in Paris. Stalin, who at this time was probably the most hated man in the world, would not trust himself to be outside the territory covered by the Red Army and so refused to come. His repressive measures against both his own people and those of the satellite states had made him a prime target for assassination and he did not trust the security arrangements of the Western powers. The conference was therefore held at Potsdam, which was within the sphere occupied by the Russian forces and Potsdam was close to Berlin, as say Rotherham is to Sheffield and anyway Berlin had been laid to waste. There was insufficient accommodation in this area for the back-up staff of the Western heads of State, so they had to attend without a number of their advisers and staff, among which of course was Virgilia, so Stalin killed two birds with one stone. He safeguarded himself and also prevented the Western Statesmen having access to their advisers and that to some degree accounts for the advantages obtained by the Warsaw pact countries in these negotiations. We were not to know this and after the trials and troubles of wartime days, I was elated at the prospect of seeing Virgilia again, after over a year of being apart.

There was of course a major difficulty. Apart from the difficulty of travel to the continent immediately after the war and the added problem of obtaining leave, we were never issued with passports. We flew over Europe and later all over South East Asia but the Air Force took care of all the paper work and provided we were careful not to enter neutral territory we were covered for all our travels. So I needed advice and gave the matter some thought. Now there were at this time four women in my life. First, there was Virgilia, of whom I have written, then my mother, whom I saw regularly when on leave. Both my parents had been in France in World War One. My father had been an infantry Sergeant and my mother a WAAC, So we had something in common - that we knew of war and it's trials and tribulations. I also had a younger sister, called Doreen, known to all as Dinah, who was a WAAF and employed as a meteorological assistant, so in close contact with aircrews. We were extremely fond of each other but due to the demands of the service, our leaves rarely coincided and our contacts were kept up mainly via our parents. It is a great regret to me that I did not write to her and establish a better relationship, as events proved we were never to be able to manage a close relationship. The fourth lady with whom I had perhaps the closer contact at this time was my father's youngest sister, my dear Auntie Mabel, whom I saw regularly. She was about 15 years older than me, she was single and was a buyer for Swan & Edgar, the large store in Piccadilly. Her speciality was jewellery and pre-war, when people could not afford to travel as they do today, her job was of such interest as by virtue of her work she had been able to travel to France and Spain, on buying trips for her firm. So she really was a sophisticated and elegant lady, who at this time had a flat in the West End and through her contacts had access to the top theatres and restaurants in London and was an ideal companion for a young and rather naive officer passing through London.

As my journeys, while on leave from Bournemouth to Sheffield, always took me through London to change trains, I was able to break the journey and get out on the town with Auntie Mabel. I had a place to stay in Whitehall, which was used by service personnel in transit and we were able to enjoy several weekends in the big city whilst en route or returning to Sheffield. So it was Auntie Mabel that I turned to for advice on this occasion. On my next leave I explained the circumstances and asked what would be my best plan. She of course quickly came up with the answer. "Virgilia is a civilian so is bound to have a passport. Why not get her leave, to come to London for a few days. I will put her up in the flat and show her around the sights until you can come over to see her." I thought that this was ideal and could not wait for Virgilia to come to London. I must point out that at this time many of the sights would be just ruins as a result of Hitlers bombing raids on London.

Life is a series of crests and troughs and I look upon this as one of the crests. I returned to base full of hopes and ambitions. I had come through the war without a scratch, my girl would soon be on her way from the states to be with me. I anticipated that I and my crew would be flying on troop carrying operations around Europe until our eventual demob. I was in for a sudden disillusion. I arrived back at Tarrant Rushton, to find the navigation leader waiting for me. We were to proceed to India in the very near future, to prepare for an airborne operation to retake Singapore from the Japanese, this was to be called Operation Zipper. As you will know, even though the war had finished in Europe, in the far east people were still suffering the hatred of war so very much. Singapore is an island, joined to the mainland of Malaya by a causeway. This causeway had to be captured and held at both ends to enable the troops to cross onto the island, hence the need for paratroops or glider borne troops to take the island end. In the event, the dropping of the Atom Bombs on Hiroshima and Nagasaki, brought the conflict to a sudden end and operation Zipper became unnecessary but we were not to know this. We did fly into Singapore but only to bring in food and medical supplies for those poor far eastern prisoners of war, that we now know suffered very badly at the hands of their Japanese captors.

We were to fly out to India in three waves, keeping the Squadron together as a unit and I and my crew were to go on the first wave. My job was to set up the navigation section which, when the final wave came out, would be taken over by the navigation leader and training for the operation would begin. Our eventual destination was a jungle strip in the control province called Raipur and the trip would take four days. A far cry from today's jet flights taking about 24 hours to Australia. We did the trip at a height of 5,000 feet, due to the limits of the aircraft which were designed for low level airborne operations.

We started to train up for Far East flying. There was much to learn, we had to tackle the navigational aids which would be available to us out there, I recall one was called Loran. In the event, few aids were practical and we were reduced to basic map reading. We would also be responsible out there for a great deal of the squadron administration, which would be much more than we had to deal with in the UK, as no specialists were available out there. This would be June 1945 and we were scheduled to fly out early in July, so we were allowed unexpected leave, I went back to Sheffield for a week, returning to base after spending my usual weekend with Auntie Mabel.

I arrived on the station on Sunday around tea time and was surprised to see a notice on the notice board saying that a telegram was waiting for me in the signals section. I immediately assumed that Virgilia had arrived unexpectedly at Southampton and was anxious to contact me. I can remember to this day, crossing to the telephone to call the section. Unfortunately it was not the expected message but a telegram from my mother telling me that my well loved sister had been found dead at her station, at Lindholme near Doncaster. A bitter blow which would change my life completely and put paid to most of the plans that

I had in mind. We were due to fly out within 10 days and I could not be released from my commitments to the squadron but I was allowed 4 days leave which allowed me to return to Sheffield to be present at Dinah's funeral. This was thanks to a lift into Bournemouth on our bomb aimer's motor bike and afterwards a quick return to fly out on the first leg of the journey to India. This first stage was a 9 hour trip to Tripoli.

Meanwhile Virgilia was now unable to come to Europe, as she had run into problems of her own. Her family appeared to be a Nomadic crowd, who were forever on the move and her brother, having just married, came up to Montreal with his new bride to see Virgilia, sadly on their way back home, they were both killed in a car accident in Texas. So she had to return to Mexico City, to be with her mother and as I was unable to say that I was destined for India until I arrived, there was a break in our correspondence. My crew and I set off for India, at 8.30am, on the 6th July, 1945, which, had she lived, would have been my sister's 21st Birthday. The operation, which today would have been carried out in a blaze of publicity, was shrouded in secrecy for reasons of security but I shall be forever grateful to the genius who arranged for our 30 WAAF's who were off duty to be placed at intervals down the runway and wave their handkerchiefs like maniacs, as we took off for North Africa. As we flew off to India, it was at a time when Virgilia and I had anticipated being together in Paris, or London. In fact we were worlds apart with me in Calcutta and she in Mexico City, so not 3,000 miles apart but nearer 10,000. It is not part of this tale to go into the adventures which awaited me in South East Asia but as far as Virgilia was concerned we had resolved that circumstances were not in our favour and with some regret and not a little distress, we had to sadly call it a day. I was under an obligation to return home where things were not going well since the death of my dear sister. Of course there were no big fast jets crossing the oceans in those days, so travelling was a very long and costly business.

I still recall the memory of those adventurous days in my life and it will always be a regret that world events prevented us from ever having a deeper and perhaps a more successful relationship.

Dear Reader,

Perhaps the story you have just read should have been entitled "What might have been". I feel we have been very privileged to be able to share in some of Geoffrey's war time memories. None of us know if Virgilia is still alive today but perhaps if she is already in paradise then Geoffrey has met up with her again. Oh but for wars so many hearts would not be broken.

To those that lived through World War Two, I urge you all to write down your memories, as Geoffrey did, for your families to know of your life in those far-off days. All I can say is, rest in peace Geoffrey and once again a big thank you for what you and your dear comrades gave for our today. Also a big thank you must go to Mary, for allowing me to write up Geoffrey's story here and I feel sure your love for Geoffrey was all he ever wished for. God bless and keep you.

Yours most sincerely,

Michael.

Chapter III

Ruth Lindner's Story

The following story comes from Mrs. Ruth Lindner, of Burwell, Cambridgeshire. What follows is the letter that Ruth wrote to me, then you will read a brief account of Ruth's hospital training from January 1939 to 1943. The story is reproduced in Ruth's words.

Dear Michael,
I must say how much I have enjoyed hearing your "War Time Memories" programmes that you do with BBC Radio Cambridgeshire's presenter, Mandy Morton. You seem to have a special way of putting people at their ease as they share their War Time Memories with you and of course with us the listeners.

I have found all of your books of such great interest and as with all true stories of life, I have found myself crying one minute and laughing the next. This was especially so with your last two books "War Time Women" and "Waving Goodbye", they really were so very true to life and brought many War Time Memories of my own life back to me, so much so that I have scribbled down some of my memories of that time in my life. I call it "Two Tired Legs" and, as you will see, I was a young nurse in those dark days of World War Two. I hope that you will be able to make a story out of it as I would be pleased for you to use it in your next book. I feel that many other retired nurses will relate to it as they recall how their legs ached after a twelve hour shift.

Two Tired Legs
I did not go into nursing with a burning desire to help humanity, so perhaps it was fate that I became a nurse. My parents had been stationed with the RAF at Seletar, Singapore from 1935 to 1937. I was almost 15 years old when we went out to Singapore and at this time, education for other ranks' children stopped at 14 years old and there was no provision for anything else at this time.

When we did return to England, I was almost 17 years of age. My father was stationed at Grantham, Lincolnshire and unbelievably now, no school would have me. I was therefore destined to take on the big wide world and say goodbye to my school days. Although, looking back, it was only the start of a life long learning process. I went on to learn short hand and typing and I took the Civil Service exam. I applied for an office job in Grantham, only to be told after my interview that they would have loved to take me on, but the last lady to hold the position had been with them for 36 years and, as I was only young, they didn't think that I would stay with them that long. I think they were right though, for how could I tell at that time how long I would have stayed with them. It was obviously not meant to be for me.

Before we went out to Singapore, we had previously lived at RAF Martlesham Heath. I decided I would write to the Matron of the East Suffolk Ipswich Hospital, to see if I could become a nurse. It was now late into 1938. I soon heard from her with a date for my interview. Following the interview, I was to have a medical and if I passed this, I was to start my training on the 9th January 1939. The doctor who carried out my medical told me that I was fine and that he could see no reason why I should not be accepted. He did go onto explain to me just what hard work it was to be a nurse, not just in all the studying one had to do, but also the job entailed much physical work as there would be a great deal of lifting to be done. It would also be very hard on my legs, for as he told me, I would have to be on them for very long days and nights. I now know just how right he was and his words have rung in my ears on many occasions since then.

When the 9th January 1939 arrived little could I have imagined that it would be the year that World War Two would start. We all had our fears of war, as people do to this day and rumours where always flying about concerning this bloke in Germany, called Hitler. Thankfully for me, my mother was now living back in Martlesham, so as I set off that day to start my new career, I was just so pleased to know that she was not too far away from me.

I arrived at the hospital, laden with my large suit case, at 6pm, it was very dark and cold. As I walked through the large front doors of the hospital, I had mixed emotions, as I am sure you can imagine. After all the formal details were sorted out I was taken by one of the maids to the junior nurses home. This maid at once addressed me as "Nurse" and she said "follow me please". As we made our way along the large corridors, which seemed endless to me, I remember that everything smelt of disinfectant, a smell that was to stay with me for years to come. Once at the nurses home I was shown to my cold little cheerless room. In the room stood an old iron bedstead and a chest of drawers on which I was told, I was allowed to put up to five articles on, but strictly no more than five. As the maid left me, she informed me that one of the nurses would be along later to show me how to make up my nurses cap. We had what we called "Butterfly Caps" in those days and there was quite an art in making them up. Our hair was supposed to be completely tucked in to the hat at all times. I well remember we had many running battles with the assistant Matron, who would wait for us at the bottom of a stair case to catch us by surprise, just to check if our hair was well tucked in. I think that over all though, we nurses won. As we soon learnt all her hiding places and would go a different way, which left her hiding for nothing.

It turned out that the nurse who did come to help me make up my hat on that very first day, had been in the same class as me at school, 4 years earlier. To meet someone that I knew made me feel much better. When she had finished showing me how to make my hat she took me off to the dinning room for dinner. We chatted about our school days together, while we each consumed a large helping of Shepherds Pie. Following this the dinning room maid came up to me and asked if I would like rice or 'tappy', as she called it, fortunately I have always loved milk puddings and I soon found that if you liked rice or tappy you certainly didn't go hungry. I think as a result I have always had good strong bones. I often think that if the prisoners of the Japanese, in the Far East, could have received the same quality of rice, instead of the slop they had to endure, many more of our dear boys would have returned home.

As I was under 18 years old, I did not go straight into the P.T.S. We were called 'Specials' and went into the children's wards. We also went on duty at 8am instead of 7am. After my first night, with very little sleep, I got up in good time and yes, struggled with my cap. A register was taken at meal times so that you could not run out. There was another young special on the children's ward, who like me, wanted to be a nurse. She was only 16 years old and her name was Kit. We are still great friends to this day, we suffered so much together in those far off war time days.

In those days everyone from Nurses, Sisters, Ward Maids, etc. lived in hospital quarters. At least we had our meals provided for us and there was always plenty of hot water to wash and bath in. By living in, we didn't waste time travelling to and from work and however hard we worked, or however bad things got for us at times, at least we had each other to talk to when we came off duty. There was a tremendous hierarchy on the wards, starting with the Sister, then Staff Nurse, Junior Staff Nurse and usually a 3rd year Nurse, followed by a couple of second year Nurses, then of course Kit and I, as the general dogs bodies. I remember the telephone terrified us, for people used large words that we had never heard of before. If we heard the phone ringing we would often hide in the sluice room, to avoid having to answer it. We got used to it in time, as one does with most new things.

I can remember that the Consultants rounds, complete with Registrar and Houseman, were just like those famous films "Doctor in the House". Only the ward Sister dare to address the Consultants.

I remember that our ward Sister was a lovely person, so very kind to us younger nurses. Sadly she was killed two years later when a land mine fell just in front of her as she was making her way back to the hospital. She had started her journey back to the hospital when, out of nowhere, came the sound of the sirens, announcing another enemy air raid. I dare say our dear ward Sister thought that she would be needed back at the hospital and that it would be safer to take shelter there. Alas this was not to be, looking back she should have taken shelter straight away in one of the community shelters, or in someone's back garden shelter, but such was her dedication that she knew she would be needed at the hospital and sadly we lost a dedicated nurse that day.

The Staff Nurse and Junior Staff Nurse, made our lives an absolute misery, for what ever we did it was always wrong in their eyes. Our only happy times were if one of these dragons had a day off. Then when the other one had her 3 hour break in the afternoon, it was just wonderful for Kit and I, not to have anyone moaning at us and making our lives hell.

The East Suffolk Hospital, was a voluntary hospital and the wards were named after people that had endowed them, such as Churchman, Cobhold, etc. In those days most people paid into the hospital scheme. It was only a few pence a week and although I do not know the ins and outs of the pre N.H.S system, it all seemed to work very well. There were very few clerical staff in those days and just a very small row of little offices. As far as I can remember no one was ever turned away because there was no bed for them. We would, if required, put up extra beds in the corridors rather than turn someone away, intensive care beds had not yet been invented.

Shortly before I had arrived at the hospital, the 90 hour fortnight had started and although it always worked out that we worked many more hours than that, it was a great improvement for all nurses. In times of crisis, we were of course expected to stay on duty longer. We received ten shillings a week and no extra for night duty, or for working on Bank Holidays. We did receive three weeks holiday a year, but this had to be taken all at once, which was not very good if it was in the middle of winter. However as most of the coast line was now out of bounds to the public, most of us just went home, or went to stay with relatives. I always looked on this time as heaven sent and would have a complete rest and catch up on my sleep. I spent one holiday in Liverpool, with my parents. My mother said it would be nice and quiet there after all the air raid sirens, which we had to endure in Ipswich. I was very lucky, for the week I arrived back from holiday, the Liverpool blitz started.

The children's ward was always special but in the winter months it was even better as it had a nice big open fire. We would sit around the fire to feed the babies. It was mainly a surgical and orthopedic ward. Several of the children had operations for T.B. of the glands of the neck. Looking back at how badly we were equipped, some of the children had quite complex operations. The only antibiotic we had was M&B 693, so far as I can recall.

We did all the cleaning ourselves, except for the floors and the hospital kitchen. Not a nurses job I hear you say, but believe me we even had to clean the brass plaques above the cots and beds, even the brass locks on the balcony doors were polished as soon as we came on duty. In the evenings we would wash all the babies woollies, clean all the dressing bowls and polish the steriliser. Then clean out the medicine cupboards and clean all the locker wheels, these were always dust traps and so had to be done often. Visiting times were very strict and restricted. The children had to be in hospital for four weeks before they could be visited, one can't begin to imagine how their poor mothers must have suffered at the time. The adult patients were allowed visitors on Saturday and Sunday and one day in the week and of course it was strictly two to a bed. With very few cars on the road in those days it was very hard for people to visit much anyway, so it certainly gave us more time to look after the patients.

My first day on the children's ward was a rather traumatic one due to the fact that during the course of feeding a little girl who had a badly fractured femur, I suddenly keeled over and fainted just as one of the surgeons arrived on the ward. I am told he just stepped over my prone body on the floor and carried on with his visit to his patient. I was sent to bed for the afternoon, but no one came to see if I was alright, so I went back to work at tea time.

Most of our time with the children was spent feeding, washing and changing them, or giving out bed pans. With several of them in plasters of one size or another, the size of the bed pan was paramount if you did not want any accidents. All the bedsteads and rubber mattress covers were scrubbed with carbolic when a patient was discharged. I must say everything was kept extremely clean and we never seemed to get the infections that you hear of in hospitals today. The "No Touch" technique hadn't come in then and each dressing was done with fresh sterile towels and dishes from a special trolley. Our hands would be washed and scrubbed in dettol, between each patient.

Apart from our two tormenters, the time went along happily in the children's ward and once I had reached 18 years of age, I went into P.T.S for 6 weeks. After all the scrubbing and cleaning that I had done this was a very welcome rest for me, as we sat down a lot. We had two lovely Sisters who were our tutors, one was quite young and the other was not far from retiring age. We had a dummy as our patient and we learned how to apply bandages and splints, as well as how to put on dressings. Of course the dummy never complained and really was the perfect patient. We also learnt about diet and vitamins, which has not changed much to this day. I soon found myself moved onto my first adult ward. This was a Female Surgical and Orthopedic ward. There were, I recall, a lot of elderly ladies with fractured femurs, of course there were no hip replacements in those days. Most of these patients were in what we called a Broomstick plaster. It must have been very uncomfortable for them as they could hardly move. There was a lot of nursing care involved on this ward, as well as washing, seeing to bedpans, caring for pressure areas. As well as cleaning dentures we had to pay attention to the patients mouths to stop them getting sores. It really was looked on as a disgrace if any patient got a bed sore and I must admit that very few did. Each patient had a blanket bath twice a week and were washed twice a day plus certain areas were washed more often, as we went round with what we called the "Back Trolley", to wash you know where.

Very soon we found that war was coming and preparations were under way. Large wooden boards were made to cover all the windows. Putting them up in the early evenings was yet another job for us. They were not only there to help the black out but they also stopped any glass flying in and hitting us or the patients, should a bomb fall close by and cause them to shatter. Plans were made to evacuate the long term patients, as we anticipated heavy air raids. Also many of our senior staff were on the reserve list, many consultants and nurses were called up for the services. Hence we lowly probationers were soon moved up the ladder and for our young age we had to take on a lot of responsibility.

Because of this, recruitment of nurses was stepped up and we had quite an influx of girls appear on the scene. Many certainly would not have thought of becoming a nurse if the war had not come along. Many of these recruits were much older than we were but they went on to make excellent nurses. Many of the new girls were clergymen's daughters.

I know that those who heard Neville Chamberlain's broadcast on Sunday 3rd September 1939, will never forget that moment in their lives, they will recall just were they were and who they were with at that time. It is as they say a moment that has marked the path of history and for those that were alive then, it is a moment they will never forget.

I was at home with my parents on that Sunday morning and heard the broadcast on their radio. After hearing it, I took a walk on my own around my parents garden and as I came to the part that was our kitchen garden, I noticed that every cabbage had been eaten by caterpillars, I remember thinking to myself "what a bad start to the war".

I was due back on duty at 2pm that day and as I returned to the hospital I remembered how worried I was about the prospect of war before the broadcast by Mr Chamberlain. Like so many others I was fearful of the unknown. Many of our older citizens had lived through the great war, but I don't think even they could imagine on this day what an horrific war was to take place. Strangely enough, now that I knew the war had started I did not feel so worried.

All this changed when the sirens screamed out and the feeling of fear overwhelmed me. We were all taken down to what passed as an air raid shelter. In fact it was the area underneath the children's wards balcony. This would have been a death trap had a bomb hit anywhere near to us, never mind a direct hit, for the balcony would have come straight down on top of us. We were all very cold and apprehensive, then a great feeling of comfort came over me when we heard it was a false alarm. I never ever went into another, so called, shelter again. I don't know why our hospital never had a proper air raid shelter as we frequently had bomber planes flying over us as they made their way to bomb Coventry or Birmingham. Most of the bombs that dropped on Ipswich, were dropped on their way back to Germany.

We saw many dog fights during the Battle of Britain period, as Martlesham was one of the enemy targets. Unknown to us at this time Douglas Bader and many of the other great flying aces, were living just over the barbed wire fence at the bottom of my parents garden.

It wasn't long after the war had started that we received our first batch of casualties, these were mainly crew and passengers from a Dutch ship called the "Simon Bolivar". The ship was on its way back from Africa and the Dutch colonies. Most of these good people had fractures of the femur, or the spine, as the ship had hit a large mine which had blown. They received most of their injuries from crashing down hard on to the deck, or hitting one of the many objects that you find on a ship's deck. I know that we only took a percentage of the patients, others went to hospitals all around East Anglia. Our empty accident ward, soon filled to over flowing. Our long stay, young male patients, who were in plaster casts, with T.B. spines, thought that these foreigners were receiving special treatment and favours, from the nurses. So much so that when the junior night nurse had her nights off, these young men would pretend to be Dutch and apparently always received their hot Horlicks, in the middle of the night. I recall one Dutch patient, a senior gentleman that we called the Colonel, had been on board the ship on his way back from service in Africa. He was used to his bottle of whisky at night and so the poor chap got the D.T's which at the time I had never heard of. We helped him through this though with a glass or two of medical whisky, this soon put him right.

We used to keep Epson salts in a jar in the ward kitchen. The sugar was kept right next to it in the same type of jar. Those on night duty always made porridge in the 'Bain Marie', it really was beautiful as it cooked slowly all through the night. One morning I accidentaly put Epson salts on all the porridge, instead of sugar. Not one person noticed and probably thought it was just some type of strange English food. I feel sure it helped them in other ways though.

One of the most unpleasant jobs at night that I am sure all nurses disliked having to do, was measuring the twenty four hour intake and output of bodily motions and keeping a record of this for each patients file. The intake side was fine but as you can imagine the output side was not so good. We had to collect it all in large enamel jars, thankfully they did have lids on them, but it really was an awful job to do. I think the worse job that we had to do was to collect sputum from people with very bad chests, the very thought of it all still turns my stomach to this day. I can well recall every time I had to carry out this task how I prayed for some handsome prince, to come and carry me away from it all. Sadly one never came.

Even with all this hard work we still had to attend lectures, given by the consultants. I wish that I had kept all my books now on Anatomy and Physiology, looking back I can see that we were taught very well by our tutors. This was all with the aid of our faithful skeleton, who used to live in our cupboard, I have often wondered who he was when he had been alive. We sometimes cursed these lectures because if you were on night duty, you were still expected to attend them at 11 o'clock and then again in the afternoon. If you had a lecture on your precious day off then you had to forsake your day off to attend the lecture. It was no good telling the powers-that-be that you lived a long way from the hospital and needed to get home as it was your day off, as you would be told that your lectures came first. We had very little money at this time, as all nurses will know, so even if we did get into Ipswich, it was only to window shop. So I dare say that our lectures kept us busy and also from spending what little money we had.

I know that there was a war on but I do feel the health of the staff was very badly cared for. During my four years stay at the hospital, I never did have a day off sick. This did not mean that there were not days when I felt like death, but as I never had a high temperature, I always had to carry on regardless. One of my friends, who was an excellent theatre nurse, spent long hours in theatre throughout the war. One day she felt so ill, she reported that she thought she had an appendicitis, this was at 10am. She was told that it was the wrong time to report anything like that now and that she should have mentioned it at 9am. Several hours later, when it was at the point of perforating, she collapsed and was rushed into theatre herself.

Our food was now all on ration and things were getting harder to obtain, we used to carry our ration of two ounces of butter and sugar around with us, for as many will recall these became our little luxuries. I would save mine up to take them home to my mother as she was on rations for one. I knew that she was very hard pressed to feed me when I went home to see her for the day. It wasn't until much later in the war that we were given coupons to help obtain food when we were on our day off. I often went home if I had three hours off in the afternoon. It was five miles to my mothers house and of course, five miles back. I would quickly change back into my uniform and get back on duty. In those days we were not allowed outside in our uniforms and I don't think it was a bad idea because there are so many germs about.

There were very few privately owned cars on the road in those war time days. At night, all road vehicles had their lights hooded. The traffic now was mainly army vehicles, which owing to their lights being hooded, had to travel very slowly. Thankfully probably because of this, we had very few road accident patients in.

I remember one group of young airmen and fitters from a nearby aerodrome, who came in to the hospital when their base was badly bombed by the Germans. These poor lads were badly injured and I remember that they were terrified every time the sirens went off to warn of an enemy air raid. Most of these lads hated taking their tablets and some time later when their plaster casts were removed, we soon found out where they had been putting them.

At this time most of our Matrons were, like us, experiencing war for the first time. From what I saw at the time, I believe that war time nursing was better done by the young nurses who certainly seemed much more flexible and more willing to help the patients. Our own Matron at this time must have gone into panic mode, for she stopped our precious nights off. We had been allowed two nights off every two weeks, which was little enough as it was. Now under her new regime we were expected to work for four weeks with no time off at all. For the first time in history we rebelled. I, of course, was one of the ring leaders and got up a 'round robin'. About thirty of us signed it and delivered it to the Matron.

There was a dreadful furore, but in the end justice was done and we were allowed to have our nights off reinstated. I must add though that we were never ever forgiven for what we had dared to do and from that day on Matron rarely spoke to us. There were no unions in those days and the Royal College of Nursing was toothless in such matters. When the unions did get going they were, I think, really for the men and were not really very helpful for us young nurses. As young nurses we had no newspapers, or radios, so most of our news was gleaned from the patients newspapers. This was usually the Mirror, as we all loved the cartoon strip "Jane". Papers were very small of course, containing about four pages in all. This was because newsprint was also rationed and of course, heavily censored. It really is only in later years that I have learned that Norwich was badly bombed during the war. All we heard at the time was that there had been enemy action over East Anglia.

My nearest encounter with an enemy plane was while on night duty, I heard a noise and looked out of the window, only to see a Swastika passing by which seemed close enough to touch. I quickly closed the drapes and thankfully he went away. I don't know what he was doing there but I thank God that he did not think we were a factory and let us have it with a bomb.

We would watch our own bombers going over to bomb Germany most nights, which really was an incredible sight. They would come from all over eastern England. Hundreds of them would fill the night skies, as they set off on their deadly raids over Germany. Needless to say when they came back over in the early morning there were never as many returning to dear old England as there had been leaving it. When I first came to live in Burwell, which is close to the American air bases of Mildenhall and Lakenheath, it was 1993 and on hearing their large planes going over head, I would often look out of my window into the sky. As I did this I would once again see all those brave British lads in their bombers, filling the night skies as they had during the war. At least I came through the war, but for so many of those brave lads, it would be their last flight.

While at this time the world was going mad with war, I had to take my preliminary state exams. These were very nerve racking affairs, with lots of subjects covered. There would also be a practical exam which included setting up trolleys for various surgical techniques. There were no ready-packed dressings or instruments, as there are today, but most of us managed to pass the prelims, as well as the state exams. As those that were nurses will recall, each hospital held its own exams as well, which were very similar to the State Prelims. Looking back now I think that many of the things we had to do were unnecessary. For instance, before an operation a large area of the patients body was washed with Ether Soap, then Ether Meths was applied followed by a pink lotion called Biniodide. Then they would be swathed in sterile towels, finished by bandages. This would be done the night before an operation and again the next morning. The Ether Soap and Ether Meth, stung the patients skin and as the poor souls had been starved as well, I would imagine it sent their blood pressure sky high. Enemas were another essential to be carried out on a surgical ward. We would often give at least nine enemas before breakfast, as it was the night nurses job to do these before they went off duty. I now know why I never felt like much for breakfast when I came off night duty. As I say these Enemas were given pre Op and again, two days post Op. We would also have several patients with colostomies, which all had to be attended to before breakfast as well. There were no plastic devices in those days to catch everything in. Some times we had to pass a stomach tube, into the patient and take a specimen of the stomach contents.

Blood transfusions were still in their infancy. The first one I witnessed was direct from patient to patient. Thankfully both survived and now that the war was here Plasma appeared on the scene, this was much easier to deal with and had a much longer life.

Of course as we did so much nursing care, we spoke to the patients a great deal. The ward sister, would also have a word with every patient, as soon as she came on duty. Bed making was one of the first jobs when we came on duty, then we treated pressure areas, did the bed pan round, took temperatures, changed dressings and served the patients' meals.

As you can imagine you could not carry out these sort of duties without speaking to the patients and because of this many friendships were struck up. Most of our wards, apart from a couple of the side wards, were arranged so that you could see every patient, from the desk, which was sited in the centre of the ward. When we had a quiet night, with no enemy raids and all the patients were asleep, we would place a shade over our desk lamp. I remember that with this nice subdued light such nights were very peaceful and calm and really were heaven sent. Another night time duty was packing the dressing drums, ready to go into the autoclave steam cleaner. There were no ready prepared things in those days, we even padded our own splints. These would all be inspected by the ward sister and if your stitching did not come up to her high standards then you really were in trouble. This work always seemed a wasted effort to us, for as soon as the splints came off the patient they had to be re-padded and made ready for the next patient to use.

We had three night sisters over-seeing the hospital in the early years of the war. They also had to check all dangerous drugs and as there were no pagers in those days, one of us junior nurses would have to run miles around the hospital looking for one of the sisters, to come and over-see the issue of drugs.

Occasionally we would have hospital dances and now and then many of the nurses would go to dances on one of the American air bases. Most of us liked these occasions, not only for the dances but also for the wonderful food there was to eat. One thing you can say about the Americans is that they always seem to eat well even if there is a war on. After all our rationing it was wonderful to feast our eyes on their smashing food.

I recall on one of these dance nights that I managed to get myself lost on the way back to the main gate, which is where we caught the bus back to the hospital. I noticed some of the American service men walking about and I was absolutely terrified as I had heard what people had said about these American chaps: 'Over here, over paid and over sexed'. Eventually a charming Sergeant took care of me and escorted me to the main gate and saw me safely onto the bus.

Evenings like this were a great escape from all the war time nursing. Around 1941 we had a dear little boy brought into hospital with very bad injuries. He had picked up a small booby trap bomb, a small type of explosive, that had been dropped by the enemy. The very bad wounds he had received to his legs were contaminated with earth and he developed gangrene. This was a ailment that so many of our lads had suffered in the trenches during the first world war. He could easily have lost his legs and his life, as so many before had. Fortunately for him nature came to his rescue. It was very hot weather and a blue bottle fly must have flown in and laid it's eggs in his wounds, because very soon there was a small group of maggots that took over, eating the poison from his wounds. When he had his plaster cast changed every few days, we all put our gas masks on, as the smell was so over powering. He was in a single room well away from the main ward, he did not seem to mind the maggots at all. Some times when I changed his bed they would be all over the place, even amongst his bed clothes. I have often thought that a little girl would not have been so happy if faced with the same situation. Because of the maggots, the boys legs were saved and he made a complete recovery. I have recently read that maggots and leeches are coming back into medical treatment, it's funny how things go round. I can recommend such treatments for cleaning out very dirty infected wounds.

As we young nurses all lived on site, we did all our studying together at nights sitting on one another's beds. One of us would usually go and prepare something to eat and we would all share it as we studied. We would ask each other questions to test one another. I don't know how they do it all today, but I am told that they do not spend as many hours on the wards as we had to. I know it may sound daft but I feel even though it was very hard work for us, our system was much better. Unfortunately the number of state exams had been cut down during the war and you also had to be 21 years old for your finals. This prolonged my training period by several months. Also if you went on to do your Midwifery, then you had to stick with it. I thought to myself what if I don't like it and decided not to study for it. Before we took our state finals, we had to take our own hospitals finals. We had recently had a new senior tutoring Sister, as our previous well loved Sister had retired and for some reason this new sister disliked us third year nurses intensely. We could never do anything right for her, she must have been so surprised, when most of us passed our exams with top marks. I must confess though that we really were very trying and for some reason we always seemed to be giggling like school girls.

It was now May 1943 and at last my training was complete. I now decided that as labour was still controlled, I would go to Nottingham General Hospital. I think I chose this as I had a few aunts and uncles in that part of the world. After a few months as a staff nurse, at Nottingham, I thought I would apply to join the Army Nursing Service so that I could really do my bit for King and Country. All field hospitals were mobilising to cross the English Channel ready for the second front at this time, although no one knew where it would be. My father was very angry with me as he was a regular Royal Air Force man and would have much preferred me to join the RAF nursing service. However, I felt that the army travelled more and was usually nearer to the front line action.

My army papers soon came through and I was to report to Chesterfield in mid March 1944. I was met at the station by a senior nursing sister and driven to an old manor house, about a couple of miles from Chesterfield. Here I met up with a group of nurses who had been serving in Northern Ireland. We were soon put through our paces by a short Scottish sergeant. I feel sure that he loved shouting at us girls and of course some girls never were any good at drill, for they never seemed to know their left, from their right. They often swung their right arm and right leg, at the same time. I still laugh when I watch the remembrance evening from the Royal Albert Hall, each November, you can be sure that someone will still do it wrong and put the others out of step.

We also had gas drill and to this day I am certain that he kept us exposed to the gas for too long. At least we had suitable large gas masks, not like those dreadful little ones that the poor civilians had to use.

We all put weight on, thanks to the stodgy army food and also because we were not working as hard as we had been in our hospital wards. We now slept four to a room on our little army camp beds. The room had bare wooden floors, with very few mod cons. As we were to be stationed at this manor house, I remember that we had to spring clean it. The army powers that be are not daft, they knew that us girls could do a better job than any bloke could at that time. It was not really nurses work, but if we moaned we were soon told "Don't you know there's a bloody war on". We even scythed all the long grass down in the gardens and dug it all ready for vegetables to be grown.

One of the girls that I shared a room with at the time became one of the first nurses to go into the Belsen death camp, when it was liberated about a year later. Needless to say she has never been able to forget the sights and smells that greeted her that day. It is so awful today when we see these camps on our televisions, but the television cannot give you the dreadful smell that was thick in the air when you walked into these camps, or the horror people felt when they saw the large numbers of vermin running around. My friend still has nightmares about the day that she entered Belsen. Today you would receive counselling both before and after you encountered such terrible things but back during the war people did not understand how such horrors could affect the rest of your life.

After all this drill and training we were scattered to various units, all over the country. I was sent to Catterick Camp, I think almost everyone in the British Army goes to Catterick Camp at some time or another. We were attached to the very large army hospital, I think this was to get us used to all the forms that you had to fill in. There is a form for everything in the army, all with a different number. There is even a form for if and when a patient dies. I was always nervous that I would forget this number, but thankfully not one of my patients died on me so I never needed to use that particular form.

One very chilly and wet morning in early June, we heard that the D Day landings had taken place. Even as far north as Catterick we heard the large number of planes that had passed over all through the night and even in the morning light the sky was still full of them.

Catterick Camp is near to Richmond, a delightful small town, with a castle on the hill. It was a hive of activity with many shops, selling every type of uniform and equipment, as you can imagine there were many army regiments, all with different uniforms, so these shops must have had a field day.

The army hospital was very different from a civilian one. Most of the patients were young men with hernias, appendices, or broken limbs. We also had a few POWs to care for, these were mainly Italians who were very cheeky to us young nurses, but they were very happy to be out of the fighting.

After a while we were posted again, this time to an ex-civilian hospital at Naburn, just outside York. We arrived at the height of the strawberry season, so we made quite a few visits to the famous 'Betty's Tea Shop' which was lovely and of course a real treat for us poor nurses. It was to be another 45 years before I returned to Betty's tea shop again and sadly for me when I did return it had lost the magic that it seemed to have during those war time days. I suppose it was due to the fact that food is so plentiful now and so it was not the same wonderful treat that it had been all those years before when food was so scarce.

In early July we were off again this time to the Hove, in the Brighton area. We were billeted in empty boarding houses, I was in one of the top attic rooms, next to the main water storage tank, so each time someone used the water there was this horrible noise of the tank refilling. It probably sounded much worse as my room was so bare, all I had was a camp bed and a canvas folding chair. The weather was very hot and our army uniform was very uncomfortable, up until November 1943 the army nurses had been in a grey and red uniform, so I think we were among the first to be in khaki, although the dresses that we wore on the wards were grey, with little capes edged with red.

We used an empty school hall for our meals, but army food was so dull, I really don't remember having any meals there. I do recall that while on our way to Hove by the train we were delayed by a tremendous blast as we were going through the London area. I think it was a V2 rocket which the Germans had started sending over about this time. These were much deadlier than the V1 rockets or doodle bugs. The trouble with these V2 rockets, was that you did not hear them coming, the first thing that you knew was when you heard the tremendous explosion. At least you could hear the V1 rockets coming, but you soon discovered that once the engine stopped it would fall and explode.

While on route to the south coast, we passed a train that was packed with black American troops, we all waved to each other as we passed. The following day our Matron called us all together to tell us what a disgrace we were to the army nursing service. She told us that she only hoped and prayed that this would all change once the war was over, because then all of the army reserve nurses would be discharged. We soon found ourselves packed off again, to the New Forest area. The New Forest was full of troops waiting to go over to Normandy. The trees in the area were a natural camouflage so we were not allowed out of the forest area and of course no one was allowed in. We knew we were not going to be kept here for too many days and one morning we were woken at 3am and ordered to report to the breakfast tent. I thought to myself "What an awful time to have breakfast", daylight was just starting to come up, when we heard the dreaded noise of a doodle bug approaching. We all shot under the long trestle tables and, thankfully, the doodle bug passed over us. As it did the engine cut out and seconds later we heard the explosion. I am afraid we did not worry about where it fell, so long as it was not on us. Once this excitement was over we were ordered to board the army lorries waiting to take us to Southampton docks.

When we arrived at the docks we saw our ship waiting for us. I remember thinking that the ship looked just the right size for us 300 nurses. However I soon discovered that we were going to be accompanied by almost 2000 troops. We soon started to wish that we wearing trousers, instead of our skirts, as we were shown down to our quarters, which were down in the bottom of the ship. I think making our way down the stairs brightened up a dreary day for many of the troops that day.

Once we were in our quarters we found that we had three tiers of bunk beds. I quickly grabbed the one nearest to the door and went off up on deck, only to find that my bunk had been taken by Matron. The only bunk left was a top bunk which was as far away from the exit as you could get, I had a very uneasy night, I can tell you. It was a very long crossing and of course we lived with the constant fear of attacks from enemy ships and U boats. It was the only time during the war that I was really frightened. To this day I cannot bear a channel crossing at night or being too low down in a ship.

I think the highlight of the trip was the American food. I recall the lovely fresh bread and the steaks we were allowed to eat. When morning came we found ourselves arriving on the French coast, at Arromanches, we docked by the Mulberry harbour, parts of which can still be seen at low tide today. This harbour had been towed out all the way from England some time before. We had to disembark in full uniform, which meant wearing our great coat and gas mask as well as carrying a full rucksack. All this equipment was very heavy, especially for young nurses, but thankfully for me a very kind young soldier took my heavy things for me. We had to climb down ladders to leave the ship, which was not very easy especially after a sleepless night.

We were soon put ashore and we climbed into lorries which drove us up the narrow twisting lanes. You could see the destruction caused by recent battles that had taken place. At this time there were very few British girls in France and as we passed our troops they would cheer and wave at us. As we passed the paratroopers they would all be singing the song, "Roll me over in the clover", we thought this a very rude song. I'm sure that today soldiers would probably be arrested or put on a charge for behaving like that, but it was all harmless fun and we took it in the spirit that it was meant.

After a few miles we arrived at a tented camp site, where we were dropped off. Here we stayed until our own field hospital was erected. I think that the British army was brilliant in equipping it's people during the war. We had a 1,000 bedded hospital acting as a casualty clearing station. Everything seemed to be there, from the operating theatre right down to the last tent peg, no item ever seemed to be missing. A lot of an army nurse's time is spent waiting for the inevitable to happen when men are fighting one another. It was lovely weather though and we were close to a dirt road that had been built by the army. Traffic poured along it day and night, taking our lads up to the front line. One young nurse, a very pretty blonde, used to sing arias from Madame Butterfly to us while we sat in the sun, watching all our lads go by.

During my stay at this camp I even received a package from one of my aunts, it was stuffed chive, a Lincolnshire delicacy. I was just about to take my first bite, when I saw that it was full of maggots. It had probably been in transit for several days and had gone off. At least I knew my aunt meant well and was thinking of me.

Eventually we were able to get to work and we started to get the wards ready for the casualties to come in. We made up the beds in the marquee that was to be our ward, each one of these had 25 beds in, so as you can imagine our hospital was made up of a lot of these marquees. I believe there were some 50 marquees in all, with about 4 of them being used as offices, a sterilising room and a staff room. The road to Bayeux was lined with these tented hospitals and was known as Harley Street by all of us Brits. I think the army had over estimated the expected casualties and I can remember talking to a cousin of mine just after the war, he had been in one of the tank regiments and he told me that the number of expected casualties was very much higher than it actually was.

Our living quarters were also tents, which were pitched in a cider apple orchard. It would have been very idyllic, if it had been in peace time. We slept three to a tent, with only our metal trunk, pushed under our camp beds, to keep our things in. At this time the water was strictly rationed to 2 pints, per person, each day. With this 2 pints we were meant to wash our smalls, as well as wash ourselves. Thankfully our uniforms went to the camp laundry. Most of the water supplies were damaged by the very heavy bombing. The rivers were all contaminated by dead cattle, it was very sad to hear the cattle crying out for water. Not that many of us felt like eating with all this going on around us but our dinning room was out in the open, the weather was very hot and so there were flies everywhere. We were allowed one bucket of cold water to wash all our cutlery and aluminum plates. You can imagine the state of this bucket of water by the end of the day. The food was plentiful but pretty unappetising. We had tinned sausage, tinned bacon - which was just like wet fat and of course good old corned beef and hard tack biscuits. I always thought that those tack biscuits were like dog biscuits, but as history shows they were a life line for soldiers over the last centuries.

Our toilets were slit trenches, with a bit of sacking put round. Fortunately, when you are young, you do not need to go to the toilet as much during the night as you seem to do when you are older. I was always worried that if I had to go during the night, I might fall into the hole. We did have one poor wandering cow, that fell in one night when looking for water. It took the Pioneer Corps, with the aid of ropes and a self made hoist, a very long time to get it out. I don't think the cow went near the slit trenches again after that, it must have learnt like us that it was not safe to wander about in the middle of the night.

The Pioneer Corps, were mainly composed of men who had come to England, from central Europe, to escape Hitler. Due to the fact that they could not qualify for any fighting services they did a variety of useful jobs, which ranged from escort duties, stretcher bearing, to all the every day tasks that needed doing. Most of these chaps were very small, but many of them were often well educated and helped us all they could.

At last our work started in earnest and I found myself with the care of a 50 bedded unit, with just one orderly to help me. He was not at all keen to work and would try all the old tricks to get out of doing anything. He had been a bricklayer by trade in peace time and probably felt out of place. Around 5pm a bugler would sound, to inform us that a convoy was arriving and sure enough most evenings they arrived just as we were going on duty. Most of these poor chaps were just so pleased to get into a clean bed and rest but those with very severe wounds went straight to the resuscitation unit. Every patient was seen and assessed by a medical officer and we would have to make out a label in quadruplet, for each one. These labels would have their name, wounds, drugs and any attention given to them. As most men were then sent home as soon as possible, the label was an easy record of their essentials. So you see it was not just our little evacuees, that these labels were used for. Penicillin had just become available for the forces and was given by injection. Those that needed to go to theatre for operations were put on a waiting list, in order of the severity of their wounds.

At one time I started to suspect that my orderly had told all the patients to ask for the bed pan or bottle during his midnight meal break, so that I would have to sort it out. I suppose it could have been that the chaps preferred me to help them, but somehow I doubt it. The disposal of the bed pan waste was very primitive and consisted of a tank situated outside the marquee. As it was always dark, you had to be very careful not to trip over the guide ropes, on the way to the tank. You can imagine what would happen to the poor nurse if this did happen.

I was kept so busy that I even had my meal breaks on the ward, I would just grab a bite when I could. Then after my first three nights on duty the powers that be decided to give me the neighbouring marquee to look after as well. This had patients with very serious chest injuries and meant that I now had 100 beds to care to. There were two medical officers with me, one for each marquee. It was impossible really for us to cope with all these poor lads, especially when I knew that on the day shifts there were plenty of staff on duty. I became so worried that one of these lads would die if I didn't have more help, that I went and spoke to the Colonel as he was doing rounds in the early mornings. I told him that it was impossible to care for our patients properly without more staff on duty at night. He smiled at me and said "Just keep doing your best". The next night we had more staff! For some reason, in most hospitals, night staff are a forgotten species and one person is expected to do what six people do in the day time.

Our casualties varied according to the kind of fighting taking place and after the fall of Caen, we went into a place called Bocage. It was a heavily wooded area with narrow lanes that had high banks on each side. Not long after we were sent here we started to receive a lot of tank casualties from all over this area. The tank crews would tell us that our tanks are not as strong as the German tanks and therefore a direct hit on one was a disaster, because it killed most of the lads inside. A lot of our casualties had very bad burns, especially to their hands and faces.

Once I finished my first stint on night duty I started on the day shift and I found myself on the burns ward. When you're only young, even though you have had training as a nurse, it can be quite a shock to see these patients. To this day I have often wondered how those lads have got on in life, for the treatment that they received in those days is nothing like the wonderful things that they can do today.

After a while I found myself back on night duty and the ward I was on often had German prisoners of war who had been brought in, badly wounded. The young ones had been told that we would kill them and so were terrified of us. The older ones knew better and really were very courageous, in spite of their very severe wounds. One night I had eight Germans brought in to me, they really were the walking wounded. They stumbled in, still wearing their camouflaged uniforms. They really frightened me, they looked so big and tall and they still had bits of tree branches sticking out of their helmets. They were accompanied by a private from the Pioneer Corps, he appeared so small standing beside them, that I could not help but laugh to myself. It would have made a wonderful cartoon sketch for any newspaper. None of them tried to escape though and they soon realised that they were now safe. However, not long after this, we discovered that one very blonde Aryan soldier was going around all the wards trying to encourage the other German prisoners to cause us as much trouble as possible. When he found that the other Germans would not follow his lead, he tried to burn down the marquee that they were staying in. Thankfully he was caught in the act and was quickly removed. I never did see him again, so I don't know where he went, or what happened to him.

I have mentioned that we were very short of water and I recall that once we had to wash eight patients in just one bowl of water. Most of them were so tired, after the fighting and the long haul in the army ambulance, that they didn't even notice how dirty the water was. Water was so valuable to us and I have often wondered what would have happened if the blonde German had been successful in setting the marquee alight, would our own boys have wasted our precious water in trying to put it out, to save the other Germans.

In time the heavy fighting moved on from our area and once Paris was liberated our troops sped on towards Belgium. We were then classed as a Base Hospital and the patients were allowed to stay longer. One problem we did have with the patients now was dysentery, as you can imagine any soldier in the front line that is suffering from dysentery is a real danger to himself and his comrades. It really is such a miserable complaint and our dysentery ward very soon became full with patients. It was not a happy marquee to be in. Fortunately a fairly new drug called Sulphaquanadine, had just arrived and was a great help to us in treating these urgent cases. If only this drug had been available to our far eastern prisoners of war as they worked on the death railway, for the Japanese. As we now know many of those men died from dysentery and they had very little in the way of medicines to help relieve their suffering.

In September 1944 a large Nissen hut was erected as nursing sisters quarters. I was glad to see the Nissen hut go up because as I was now a sister it would mean that I would not have to live under canvas any longer. Thankfully it contained a shower and now that the water shortage had been resolved, this became a great luxury. None of the other medical staff were allowed to use our shower unless they were a guest of one of us. We girls soon acquired quite a following from our male colleagues, who we knew only really wanted to use our shower, but we still enjoyed the attention.

By now we were given the occasional day off and as Bayeux was only a few miles away this became our favourite venue. It had escaped most of the damage from the fighting and so still looked a nice place. The Lion D'or hotel was a favourite haunt, it was where the war correspondents all gathered. I was to return there many years later in the 1960's but by then it had declined and, for me it's magic had all gone. It has now gone completely, replaced by a high rise block. They call it progress!

On one of my days off I went as far as Caen, it was literally a pile of rubble due to the heavy bombing. Only the church bore any resemblance to its former self and probably became the heart of a whole new town when it was rebuilt.

In early October 1944 we were all moved off to Brussels and another unit took over our tents and Nissen hut in Normandy. It was a gruelling two day journey for us, in the back of back breaking army lorries, we only had wooden benches to sit on. We stopped for the night at a place called Poix, were we slept in what had once been an old German barrack block. We had no mattresses, but we were all so tired that we did not even unroll our bedding, we just fell asleep on the iron slats of the beds. The next morning we could hardly move with our aches and pains, caused by the long journey sitting on those old wooden benches and the night we had just had trying to sleep on iron bed slats. We did look a sorry lot. We helped one another up onto the back of the lorry and set off again. Our toilet stops were along the road side, girls went to the right and the boys to the left. Believe me this was much better than the filthy French toilets. By the time we reached Brussels I was lying flat out on my back on the floor of the truck, such was the pain coming from my back. We were so glad that we had arrived and it really made us realise how our army lads had suffered as they were moved around, and they had to fight the enemy as well.

Here we were in a large Belgian hospital, which had a good nurses home with separate rooms for all of us. The other luxury we had were bathrooms and we girls thought we were in heaven because the baths were so deep. We soon had them full of lovely hot water and soaked in them to ease our aches and pains. As we did this we could see the dirt and black grime, coming out of our pores. It felt so good to feel really clean, it made us feel like women again, but the best thing of all was that our rooms had locks on the doors. It was just heaven to be able to be on your own for a change, just close the door and shut the world out.

I was put in charge of a large mixed surgical ward, with plenty of water and all mod cons, this made life so much better. Brussels was a lively city in those days, full of cafes and night clubs, all no doubt cashing in on all the troops passing through. One evening we girls got into a bit of bother when we mistook a brothel for a café. Thankfully a very polite local informed us that it was not a café and that it was not really the sort of place for nice girls to be seen in.

The local people were very short of food during this time and I feel sure that many a tin of corned beef changed hands between our boys and the local ladies of the night. There were very few young Belgium men around as most had been shipped off to be used as slave labour by the Germans.

Around Christmas time, 1944, we had some dreadful weather, with fog and heavy snow, it was very cold. The Germans made a desperate counter offensive later named 'The battle of the Bulge'. I was on night duty at the time and, when all was quiet on the ward, we could hear the German guns barking out. For a while they were advancing through the Ardennes and back into Belgium. A lot of American troops were sent in to stop the advance, they all looked as if they were new recruits. Poor chaps would not have known where they were, for most of the area was pine forest, with snow and quite often fog. I dare say many of them died without ever firing a shot. I found out later that plans had been made to evacuate us nurses should the worst happen and the Germans made it through to us. Rumours were rife of course, as paratroopers were dropping very near to us. In fact the last squadron of German planes to be seen over Brussels was around New Years Day. Thankfully though, they never dropped any bombs but not long after New Year, the V.1 rockets started to drop on Brussels, sending many of the locals into mass hysteria.

We had a few civilian casualties come into our hospital and I think the worse job we now had was trying to calm their relatives down when they visited them. They certainly were very different from the good old stout British people. As well as these local casualties, we also started to get many of our own poor lads coming in. Some were badly wounded from stepping onto land mines left behind by the Germans as they retreated. Their injuries were always very sad to see and many resulted in the loss of part, or all, of a limb. The poor chaps were always very upset when they came round from the anaesthetic to find that they

Arthur Seager in his Army uniform

Ruth Lindner (far left) in the children's ward at Christmas

Joan Walton at the VES concert party

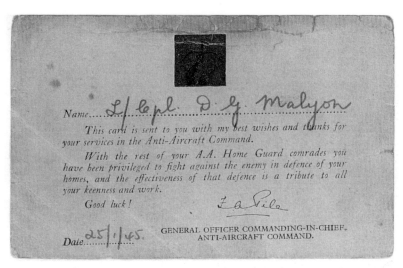

*D. G. Malyon's card of recognition and thanks
upon leaving the Home Guard*

Joan Walton and the Steel City Stars

Rosalind Martin

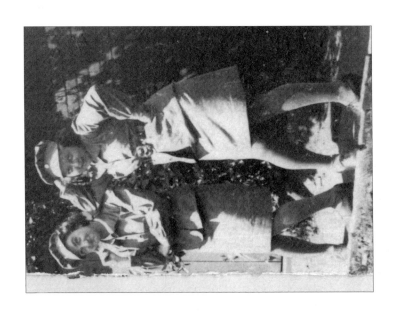

Joan Walton and friend

had lost a leg or a foot, especially as it was now so near to the end of the war.

I know that in early 1945 we had several self inflicted injuries come in. These chaps were just at the end of their tether. Many of them had seen their best mates killed in front of them and they had just broken down and become physical wrecks. It was very sad to see these chaps, men who had given their all, resort to this. Thankfully in Brussels, we had far better ward orderlies than in Normandy, in fact any that were difficult were sent along to me to deal with. One I well remember had no intention of working but he was a wonderful entertainer and, as we had a piano on the ward, I let him entertain the patients. He was a Londoner and much like Max Bygraves, I feel sure that he was better than any medicine we could give out because he really did lift their spirits. One of my best orderlies came from Norfolk, his surname was Duffield and I still wonder where he is today.

By the end of March 1945 the fighting in the deserts of the world was finished and some of the sisters from these desert hospitals joined our staff. Many of them had been in the army for years and were therefore senior to us and took over our wards, which as you can imagine did not please us at all.

We were still receiving many casualties, especially when our boys crossed the Rhine. A lot of large gliders were being used at this time to bring our troops over and many of these made crash landings, which resulted in many casualties with injuries ranging from fractured spines to broken legs. However we started to feel that victory was now in sight and home leave started. I found myself going in a plane for the first time in my life and it was a great worry to me. It was an old Dakota which had none of the modern amenities you find in aircraft today and it seemed very cold and slow. One of these had been shot down just three weeks earlier while taking others home on leave, so I think I had every right to be worried. I had my head in a bag for most of the journey home to Croydon. When I returned after my leave I think it was even worse, for the turbulence was very bad. I know that I never went on another plane until many years later, in fact it was 1982.

The 108 B.G. Hospital, was now breaking up and our job was coming to an end. Many of my fellow nurses went out to India, to do their best for those that had suffered so much in the far east. Others went on into Germany. Many years later my husband and I returned to France and Belgium and we found the site of the old 108 British General Hospital. There was just a little strip of tarmac left where once the entrance to the hospital had been and there were still a few strands of barbed wire in place. The fields around all looked barren and neglected and the whole area looked depopulated. We called at a little farm house where we nurses used to have the occasional glass of cider. The elderly couple that lived there were delighted to see us and got out a bottle of their best wine, to share with us. They told us that in all the years that had passed since the war we were the only couple who had visited them, in spite of the fact that a field hospital had been in the field adjoining their house. Perhaps for so many others their memories of this place were not ones that they wanted to revisit in person. We recalled what happy memories we could of that time. We even talked about the first Normandy wedding of the war that took place. This was led by our dentist, who played the bagpipes. I know it was all featured in the popular magazine of the time called the Picture Post. I myself found it very sad revisiting all the old haunts, places where so much had happened for us girls in those nightmare days of World War Two. The now empty beaches were quite heart breaking, to say nothing of the cemeteries. They were not as vast as those of World War One, but once again the head markers showed the young age of those that had given their today for our tomorrow. Their ages ranged from eighteen to about twenty eight years old. Twenty eight seemed quite elderly, as there were so many showing a young age.

After the war I returned to the East Suffolk Hospital for a while. I was welcomed back by all the medical and nursing staff that I had worked with throughout the early years of the war. In those days in hospitals you knew the entire staff, from the maids, porters, up to the top consultants. I was still at the East Suffolk when the National Health Service came into being. In our hospital one of the first things they did was to cut down an extensive and beautiful Wisteria that covered several yards of the front of the hospital, soon afterwards they cut down a magnificent tree, need I say more.

I mentioned before how one of my best friends was one of the first nurses to go into Belsen when it was liberated. The pictures we see on tv and films, are still horrific, but they can be nowhere near as bad as actually being there. I know the sights she saw are still etched in her memory after all these years. It is said the Germans, had about 100 of these concentration camps, most of us only know the names of a few. Although I myself did not see any of them, they have lived with me all my life. On a cold winters morning when I am tucked up in my warm bed, with my electric blanket and the central heating on, I often think of those poor souls that were starving in such flimsy clothing, as they were dragged out into the bitter cold for roll call. Then to face a day of slave labour, before it was their turn to go to the gas chamber. Death really must have come as a blessed relief to them. Looking back on it all, one can not help but relive ones own war time memories. My hope would be that this century we will see peace and happiness for all, where ever people may live and by whatever creed, so that the sacrifices made by so many people will not have been all in vain. I must admit though as I look at our world today, I sometimes wonder.

To finish my story I would like to tell you about one of my happy war time memories. This would be the wonderful Christmases we shared in the hospital. The wards were always so beautifully decorated, there always seemed to be someone amongst us who was very clever at doing that sort of thing. The patients were not sent home as they seem to be today, nursing staff were all on duty. There were no married nurses then, so our only obligation was to our patients. The carols, sung by the doctors and nurses, as they went round all the wards, were so very moving. The Ministry of Food gave us a few extra rations for Christmas, which was a great treat for all. One of our sisters was in charge of the kitchens and she worked very hard at preserving all the fruit and vegetables that we had been given by the local churches at Harvest Festival time. Each patient received a small present in their Christmas stocking and were very happy that visiting hours had been extended. It really was such a special time and when I think of all that was going wrong in our world at that time it showed me just how lucky I was. They really were some of my happiest Christmases and to this day are treasured as my happy 'War Time Memories'.

●

Dear Ruth,

Thank you for sending, as you say, your scribbled notes to me of your War Time Memories, I hope that you are pleased with the result. I have enjoyed writing your story and am proud to feature it here. As I was writing up your story, today's media were reporting on how the Matron may soon return to our hospitals. I first heard it on the news, just as I sat writing about your memories of the Matron. Perhaps you had better come out of retirement and become one of our modern day Matrons.

I feel that, like me, my readers will see that you and your comrades gave your best to care for our brave lads who suffered such horrific wounds in battle. Also the love and care you gave to those dear little children who came into your care, for they must have been terrified at being away from their mothers during their stay in hospital. I am sure that the love you showed them during that time has stayed with them in their memories. Nursing really is a calling and I say thank God that you never took that office job in Grantham. Thankfully you heard the call and became one of our angels here on earth. I, like so many others, call you angels for you really do Gods work, as you all care for others that are ill and suffering. As you will know I raise funds for Breast Cancer Research and through this I meet many ladies that are suffering from breast cancer. I wish you could hear the good things that they say about their nurses to me. Thank you once again for allowing me to write up your story which I hope other nurses will also find of great interest.

Chapter IV

Walter Adams's Story

I met Walter at one of my talks which I gave to his group at the Village College, in Cottenham, a village not to far away from where I live, in Cambridgeshire

I started my talk with a recording of Neville Chamberlain's speech to the nation on the 3rd September 1939. After the talk Walter came up to have a chat with me. The first thing he said was "I can remember just where I was, all those years ago, when I first heard that speech". I told Walter of how so many people tell me that, many still re-live that feeling of shock when they hear it again.

Walter went on to tell me of the friendships that he made while serving his King and Country and of how he still treasures the memories he shared with those friends so long ago.

A few days after my talk Walter sent me the following story, as his tribute to his dear old friend Stanley. As you read this story you will discover that Stanley and his friend Tubby, gave their regiment much to remember them by.

A Partner in the Dance of Fate

Sunday, 3rd of September, 1939 arrived. It was a lovely, sunny and warm day. There were no church parades, they had been abolished some time before; those who wished to go to church did so on their own. At 11 o'clock we all gathered around the radio in the barrack room to listen to Mr Chamberlain's speech. His measured and musically modulated voice, with its polite, reserved and civilised tones, stated succinctly and almost reverentially, that we were now at war with Germany. There were a few moments of silence and then, without comment, we all drifted away to our own bed spaces. Soon the silence was shattered by the usual wry and noisy quips that such momentous occasions bring forth and within minutes everyone was chatting away quite happily, almost as if it were a cricket score that had been announced. Young men, particularly soldiers, have an urgency for life and must get on with it. Someone switched the radio to something more lively, probably to Radio Luxembourg, the pop station of that day and, almost on cue, two of the bandsmen started dancing together, one pretending to be the Colonel and the other the Colonel's Lady. The Colonel was small and dapper with a neat Ronald Colman moustache; his Lady was much taller. Their impression was grotesquely lifelike, the dialogue funny; their gyrations over the wax-polished floor, in and around the beds, provoking gales of laughter despite this being their regularly presented party piece.

For some reason the scene and the atmosphere etched itself on my mind. Possibly, it was the juxtaposition of events, the serious followed by the frivolous or, perhaps it was simply because I had been away from barrack life and its humour for the past year, consequently it had a certain freshness and sharpness about it. Whatever the reason, while I was enjoying the fun and joining in the laughter, I felt at the same time that this was all taking place outside of myself, almost as if it were happening elsewhere and that I was merely a distant spectator. I saw Sydney and Tubby, who was no longer tubby, his nickname had been acquired several years before on enlistment, doing their Waltz-Foxtrot-Tango routine. I saw the row of army beds, the circle of amused faces and noted, with an almost superficial detachment, that Sydney was, in reality, a superb ballroom dancer, although now pretending to dance, as many officers in those days did, as if they had two left legs, both wooden; and that Tubby, for all his meek diffidence as a person and his very average competence as an instrumentalist, had a superb sense of parody, all the more surprising because it was so unexpected. They always performed their act spontaneously: they gravitated together in some chance fashion at the exact moment the right music was being relayed and before we knew it and probably before they knew it, they were dancing and it was the Regimental Ball! They performed their act as much to indulge themselves as to entertain us: it gave them an opportunity to exercise a talent that normally had to remain dormant and submerged.

I had seen their performance many times previously, but this occasion it appeared to have a special significance beyond that of its occurrence and it was not until almost a year had passed that this was made known to me. The following day we were involved in the 'Battle for France'. The whole battalion was on the line of march carrying out one of the many defensive sideways and backwards steps of the retreat that would end at Dunkirk. We were marching in staggered formation along both sides of a road, built on an embankment through a long valley, which was being shelled by a long-range gun aided by a spotter-plane. Some of the shells would land short and send small clods of earth exploding upwards; others would drop on the far side of the embankment; the odd one would land on the road itself. One of these wounded Sydney. As the shells crashed down, the column of troops would bend down and rush forward as if to dive for cover but there was no cover; yet, it was hard to resist the temptation to rush forward and break the extended formation which alone would keep casualties to a minimum.

One of our Company Commanders, a World War One veteran, walked up and down the road, swinging his walking stick, as if he was out on a Sunday stroll, encouraging the troops more by his seemingly carefree attitude than by anything he said. As a platoon sergeant leading his men, I tried, in a small way to emulate his example and kept a regular pace with what I hoped was an unflinching manner and an unworried face, although as I heard the crump of shells exploding around me, my stomach would shift into over-drive. It was a long march, but the flow of adrenaline which accompanied our fear spurred us on until, eventually, we were safely out of range of the guns and the light began to fade.

A vivid memory of this march was of an ambulance, crowded with wounded soldiers, being driven past us in the centre of the road just as a shell landed about thirty yards further up the road. The wounded, all covered with blood-soaked bandages, could be seen in their panic trying to get out of the ambulance, but the door was fastened shut. The driver ignored all this, he just hooted his horn at the troops forward of his vehicle and drove on. I didn't envy him his job. I preferred to take my chance on the line of march.

The following November, just over a year after war had been declared, found me at the Regimental Training Centre and those of us who were musicians in the Regimental Dance Band were playing in the Town Hall of the local city for a Tea Dance in aid of war charities. During one of the dances, I spotted a familiar face at the side of the dance floor; it was Sydney making his way towards the stage where the band were playing. He stood there, watched and listened and later sat in and played the trumpet. He was as spruce as ever, immaculately dressed, his Ronald Colman moustache neatly trimmed and managing his artificial leg so well it was difficult to believe a shell had taken it off on that long march in France, the previous May. During a rest in a chorus of one of the dance numbers, I turned to him and saw that he was watching, with an appreciative eye, the dancers circling and swirling around the dance floor below us. As I looked down, following his gaze, I saw superimposed on the swaying figures, the barrack room at Plymouth and there were Sydney and Tubby performing their 'Officers Ball' routine as they did on that Sunday morning when war was declared.

Dear Walter,

Thank you for sharing with us your War Time Memories. I am so glad that my talk was able to evoke happy memories of your dear pals, Stanley and Tubby. As you know, such characters are priceless when the chips are down and as we can see, Stanley never let the loss of a leg hold him back. He really was a true entertainer.

Best wishes,

Michael

Chapter V

Constance Ronan's Story

The following story comes from Mrs Constance Ronan, of Groombridge, East Sussex. I know that Constance's story will bring many memories back to those of you who were evacuees during World War Two, as well as all my dear ex Land Army Girls. As you will read Constance, like so many in those dark days of World War Two, had her share of heart ache, thankfully she came through it all and shares her story with us here now.

When the war started I was a girl of thirteen years old and lived in Mitcham, Surrey. The first noticeable effect the war had on us was the start of rationing. Three ration books were issued, one for children under six years old, one for people over six years old and a special travellers book for those people who travelled around the country. The first food items to be rationed were: butter, sugar, bacon and ham. The weekly allowance was 4 oz of butter, 12 oz of sugar and 4 oz of bacon and ham, per person. You would take your ration book to the shopkeeper and he would stamp it and give you your allowance of food for that week.

By March 1940 all meat was rationed and each person was only allowed 1 shilling and 10 pence worth of meat, 9p in today's money. Children under six were allowed 11 pence, 5p in today's money. By July, tea was rationed to 2 oz per week, as was margarine. The sugar ration was cut to only 8 oz per week.

In 1941 a points system was introduced. People were allowed 16 points per month. They could then buy so called luxury foods, such as dried fruit, biscuits, cereals, tinned fish or tinned meat.

In 1942 dried eggs appeared in the shops and we were allowed one packet a week which was the equivalent of twelve eggs. There was very little fresh fruit and no fresh eggs. Sweets were also on ration and only 12 oz of sweets every four weeks was allowed. The sweetie coupon was highly prized by the children.

When the bombing started in London children were evacuated to the country, this of course meant leaving their homes and their mums and dads. When the time came for us to leave home we were taken to the nearest train station; where we met up with our friends from school. Our destination was to be Cranleigh in Surrey.

As we boarded our train there were, of course, lots of tears within the families. We were given little tags with our names on so that we could be easily identified and we had to take our gas masks in case of gas air raids.

When we arrived at Cranleigh we were taken to the local school were the ladies of the village were waiting to see who they would give homes to. Unfortunately, when I was a child I had eczema very badly and my arms and leg were bandaged. I did look a very sorry sight and when all the children had been chosen, I was left on my own with my teacher who took me to stay with her for the night. In the morning we finally found a lady who would give me a home.

The lady appeared to be kind, but that all changed when we got back to her house. I discovered that, as well as me, she had given a home to four other children. I was the odd one out as they all came from a different school to me and all knew each other. The lady of the house made me do all the washing, ironing, making of beds as well as all the other housework. I was a Cinderella and I was so unhappy that I wrote to my mum and told her of all that I had to do and she came and took me home. I could not go to school, as by now they were all closed, so my mum tried to teach me as best she could at home. It was very frightening living back in Mitcham; the air raid siren would wail out a horrible sound, to let us know the enemy planes were on their way and we had to get into the air raid shelter as soon as possible. The shelter was in the garden and was a small brick building with very thick walls which made you feel quite safe when you were inside. We would take a flask of tea and some food in with us and we had 2 bunk beds just in case the air raid happened during the night.

We heard the planes fly above us and just prayed we would be kept safe. One night an oil bomb exploded outside our house which left a huge crater and smothered everything in oil. Later we were hit by four incendiaries which were small bombs that caused fires and we also had an unexploded German bomb fall in our back garden.

I remember climbing into the loft to help my father put the tiles, blown off during the bombing, back in place. It was a very sad time for everyone. My mother, father, sister and I were the only ones living along our road. We used to see a policeman and an ARP Warden now and again but that was all.

When I was 15 years old I experienced the saddest day of my life. My mother was killed by a bomb which hit our house. My father and sister were taken to hospital but they were not seriously hurt. I had left the house just half an hour before the bomb landed. I was absolutely devastated. I thought the world of my mother and it took years to get over the shock, especially as it happened so suddenly.

The war was a very cruel time for lots of people. After my sister went into the Land Army I had to look after my father. My father was a very cruel man and he had treated my mother very badly. I never really forgave him for that.

In 1941 I left school and went to work in Harrods. I worked in the Music Department and it was a very interesting job, I served many famous and important people, including a few film stars.

When the friend I worked with left Harrods to join the Women's Land Army she wrote to me and asked me to join. When I was old enough I left my job and went and joined her on the farm. Strangely enough the farm was in Ewhurst, the village next to Cranleigh where I had been evacuated to. My uniform consisted of: 2 beige shirts, 1 green tie, 1 green pullover, 1 pair of strong brown shoes, 1 very warm three quarter length overcoat, 1 pair of dungarees, 1pair of strong wellington boots, 2 pairs of woollen socks and a hat, which I could never keep on my head.

On the farm where we worked my friend Rosemary looked after the horses and I looked after the chickens and turkeys and helped for 2 days each week in the cow sheds. When I joined the Land Army I did not know anything about chickens or turkeys but I soon learnt.

I loved my life in the country, up at the crack of dawn then up into the woods to let the chickens out of their houses. They would all come flying out as if there were no tomorrow.

The farmer kept a big copper vessel in the woods and I used to throw lots of potatoes in there to cook then I would break them up and scatter the pieces for the chickens to peck at. They really enjoyed that. The chickens also ate ground meal which I used to carry on my back in a sack up to the wood at about eleven o'clock each day.

On my first day I was carrying the sack with the old cart horse following me behind. What I did not realise was that he had taken a nibble out of the bottom of the sack. By the time I got up to the wood there was precious little meal left, so I had to go all the way down again to get another sack and do my journey all over again. I made sure that was the last time that ever happened.

I grew very fond of my chickens, especially when I put their eggs into the incubator and seeing the hundreds of little yellow chicks looking at me when I opened it later and pulled out the trays it was wonderful.

The turkeys were kept in a very large hut and I used to let them out at about eleven o'clock in the morning and round them up again at around four in the afternoon. I used to whistle at them and they would come to me just like dogs. However, I did prefer my chickens although, sometimes it used to take ages to collect the eggs as many of them used to hide them in the straw by the haystack

I lived in a dear little bungalow which was joined to the farm house. It had a super bathroom. The other Land Army girls were billeted in the village and had to make do with an old tin bath brought in from outside and placed in front of the fire. They would take it in turns to come to my bungalow for a luxury bath.

People seemed more honest in those days. When the time came for weekend leave, I would cycle to the station, leaving my bike in a ditch and when I came back on the Sunday I could pick my bike out of the same ditch and then cycle like mad back to the farm. This was all done in the pitch dark as we were not allowed to use any lights in case there was an air raid.

I was very lucky to be able to eat with the farmer and his wife. The food was great, there was always fresh eggs and plenty of milk. They were wonderful people, always very kind to me and I was a very happy and contented girl.

When I was twenty I left the Land Army and came home to look after my father. I got engaged to my boyfriend, Bernard, who was a Petty Officer in the Navy.

On Bernard's next leave we got married and in the years that followed we had three children, Susan, my eldest, Philip and then another girl, Annette. Now I have 11 grandchildren. Sadly, 12 years ago, after a wonderful marriage, my dear husband passed away with cancer. I nursed him at home with the help of my daughters. My family were never far away when I needed them and they are all very good to me. They keep a special eye on me. I live on my own in a village called Groombridge, in East Sussex, I have a lovely little bungalow and I have lots of friends here, I still love animals and I can often be seen taking other people's dogs out for walks.

Dear Constance

Thank you so much for sharing your War Time Memories with me and for allowing me to use it here in my book for others to share. I really am so grateful that your daughter, Susan, told you about my books and even more grateful that she made contact with me and put us in touch with one another. I dare say that after working in Harrods and serving all those high class people, as well as all the film stars, it really did come hard when you first became a Land Army Girl. I know from my talks with my many ex Land Army friends, that they would have loved to have had your luxury bathroom instead of the old tin bath, put in front of the kitchen range. They tell me that at least three of them would have to share the same water, still they say they were happy days. I think the part of your story that touched me most was the sad loss of your dear mother and the part that made me smile was how you would leave your bike in the ditch when you went home for the weekend and that it would still be there, safe, when you returned days later. Don't try it today Constance, but I think I can see why so many people, when they look back, call them happy days. Kind regards,
Michael

Chapter VI

Alice Stokes's Story

The following story comes from Mrs. Alice Stokes, of Harlow Essex. Alice, shares with us her 'War Time Memories' as a little evacuee of World War Two. It is a story that would have featured well in my last book 'Waving Goodbye' and is one that those of you that were also evacuees at that time, will really relate to.

A childhood memory

"The end of an era" I thought, as the sad news came of Harry's passing. That was the end of my childhood experience. It was hard to imagine that I would never stay in that house any more, after fifty two years of it being my home. Never to walk up that garden path, lined with tall sunflowers, hear the babbling brook running by the house, entering through an ever open door, which led straight into the front room, gleaming with brass and no more to be welcomed by that smiling face again. Dear Harry, Mrs Cook and Ruby . All gone. They played a very important role in my life, through the errors of war.

We were a poor family living in the east end of London. I was born in Islington. My parents named me Alice after an aunt who had died of cancer. It seemed I had rickets as a baby and ended up in Carshalton hospital for a year. Afterwards I stayed with an aunt Lizzie and uncle Charlie (who used to tickle me with his moustache) in Chingford. "Talked with my eyes", they would say. This early part of my life is pretty vague but it was to become most memorable. Mum and Dad had five children at the time war broke out: myself, my elder brother and my sisters Marie, Rene and Ann, We all lived in a three-bedroom flat in Homerton, opposite the Hackney marshes. A pretty dreary existence, with the smoke, the poverty and the dismal blocks of flats towering above us.

The time for our evacuation came in 1940. I remember wearing a gas mask encased in a cardboard box and a label pinned to us. Paddington station with the hissing steam train and crowds of children with Mums and adults seeing them off to God knows where, still remains vividly in my mind. I was to go with my sister Rene, three years my senior. Saying goodbye to my Mother seems to have faded in my memory. We had never seen a train let alone travelled on one. Our destination was unknown so we must have felt very confused, not knowing what lay ahead. The actual journey seems to have been blocked out of my mind and the next thing I remember is being placed in a cottage, in a very quiet lane in the west country, with Mrs Cook and Mr and Mrs Sully. They had no children of their own, so we would be a challenge to them. "Are we going home tomorrow" I said to Rene. She probably fobbed me off with some kind of answer which I can not recall. This quaint, primitive cottage with lamps, candles, no running water or bath, an outside toilet - which was a wooden seat with a hole and underneath a running brook. Water was drawn from a tap at the end of the lane which had to be carried to the house in buckets. I can see myself staggering, red faced, carrying galvanised pails of water. We would carry a candle up to bed, to light our way to the pitch black bedroom. The only consolation was to climb into a soft feather bed and sink into oblivion. We settled into our billet after a few weeks quite nicely and were being taught a new way of life. We were being brought up in a proper manner to mind our P's and Q's; taking our shoes off before going upstairs; asking to leave the table. I had the habit of staring at people and was promptly checked every time. In spite of all the little disciplines, a sense of belonging surrounded us.

Mr Cook was a small, chubby man and he used to call me 'titch'. I was very tiny for my age and had very short, black hair with a fringe, which enhanced my large brown eyes. Mrs Cook was a lovely lady, with long, grey hair, twisted into a bun and fastened with hairpins. I had a fascination for meddling with hair, hence the longing to be a hairdresser when I grew up. Mrs Sully, Ruby, was Mrs Cook's daughter. She was very neat and fussy. Everything had to be in it's place. In spite of her fussiness, she was very sweet and she was a super cook. Mr Sully, Harry, was mostly away fighting in the war but came home on odd occasions. His kit bag always interested me and I was always curious to find out what he had in it. I recall the night he came home, with his kitbag slung over his shoulder, waking us up. I can still visualise Mrs Cook sitting up in bed, drinking a glass of whiskey, in the middle of the night. So exciting! One day on arriving home from school, I vaguely remember everyone sitting around very quiet, looking very sad and, although I didn't know why, I also felt a great sense of loss. I later discovered that Mr Cook had died and was laid out in the best room. It is difficult now to recall all the details. We had not been there very long and I seem to only be able to recall certain outlines of the early days.

We settled in nicely and soon became accustomed to a different lifestyle entirely. The feeling of security and warmth was soon ours. The attachment of belonging grew. Everyday we walked a mile to school, passing the cemetery, where they are all buried now. The school was a building made of Wedmore stone and covered with creeping ivy. Our classes were made up of children of different ages. The headmaster, now that I look back, was a little perverted. At the time nobody dared say anything. He was also a beekeeper and I can see him now with his head and face protected by a mesh contraption. He was always scratching his rear! He loved to read particular quotes from the Bible, which were a bit rude and rub his hands up and down the girls legs, while marking their books. It is only now that I realise the implication of it all. He passed away a few years ago.

My Mother wrote to me now and again. She wasn't very good at writing letters and was bogged down with the war. My Father suffered from ill health and now they also had two more children to cope with. Jean died of a brain tumour at nine months old, which meant Ronnie, the youngest now and Ann, stayed with Mum and Dad during the blitz. The rest of us had been evacuated. We were not aware of the blitz taking place in London. We were well protected from the bombings and atrocities and were oblivious to such things. Many relatives of Mrs Cook seemed to die while we were there and these were not very pleasant times, but life went on.

When I look back, I realised that my sister and I delighted in the simpler things of life. Going to bluebell wood, where my fairies lived, used to be the highlight of our day. Picking blackberries, with our little lace-up boots on and carrying big wicker baskets and a crook, was another. Painting, writing and reading were also favourites. Long country walks on Sundays to a relations for supper, was an ideal way of spending a day.

The vintage pickles with a lovely spicy taste was heaven. The adults would drink cider on tap. We would then walk home in the pitch-black darkness, along hedgerows and fields. One night we heard a great moaning, coming from one of the ditches and I nearly jumped out of my skin! We could hardly see a thing in front of us and so we assumed it was a drunk, who had fallen into a ditch. I suppose we probably walked about six to eight miles in an evening. On one of these evenings, we were observing a strange object in the sky, we all started to panic and run but it seemed to follow us. We later learned that it was a barrage balloon and we have laughed about it ever since.

We grew to love the family we had acquired. A mutual fond relationship was developing. They were raising us as their own. I remember Christmas times so vividly. We often went carol singing, calling at houses, giving our rendering of a few carols and afterward being invited inside to sing, which was often rewarded with some sweetmeats. How we went around in the darkness, still surprises me. On Christmas Eve we would hang up our stockings; one for Mrs Cook, one for the cat and then our own. The excitement now mounted! Then on waking we eagerly claimed our full stocking sitting at the end of the bed. The contents consisting of an apple, an orange, books and a paintbox. I would content myself with reading and painting all day. Those were very happy memories of such times. We appreciated everything and fully indulged ourselves all day. Dinner would consist of either duck or goose, with all the trimmings and we devoured the meal with great relish, I loved my food. Although I was very small for my age I ate everything and always had room for second helpings. Despite my dislike of vegetables, as well as cheese and milk at first, I soon acquired a taste for almost everything, except cheese.

Within a short time, I soon picked up the famous Somerset accent and passed as one of those 'country' girls quite quickly. I did wonder why I was addressed as 'me son' considering I was a girl! I soon became very fluent in this new language. When I returned to London a few years later I was accused of speaking 'posh'. I rolled my R's and broadened my words admirably. I was able to hold my own with all the local girls. Now I had become a fully fledged villager.

Sunday school was the rule of the day. In our seersucker dresses, panama and patent shoes, we would parade off to the chapel. During the service we might be chosen to sing a hymn. Although I was nervous, I would always oblige and to this day I still like to sing - one of my hobbies now is entertaining the elderly. The doctrine was simple and enjoyable and was the grounding for the faith I have today.

Sunday lunch was the next thing on the menu and of course was gratefully received, always preceded by our mealtime prayer. The rest of the day was taken up with reading, playing board games, having tea and going for one of our famous walks. On nights like these it was a pleasure to jump into bed. The countryside appealed to me greatly and still does. I loved the openness, the freshness, the tranquillity, the aroma and the sunny days - especially the sunny days. Those days when Mrs Cook and Mrs Sully would go out for the day and we would have to let ourselves in with the key, left under the door mat. A dazzling white cloth would be covering the finely chopped sandwiches and sweetmeats arranged on the table.

These would be devoured ravenously. Always on lovely, hot summer days it seems. After having our fill, we would close the door very carefully and put the key safely back under the mat.

As time went on we became more and more part of the village and of course this was our home and nothing could disturb our peace. But alas that was not to be. One weekend my Father came to see us. As we hardly knew him we found his visit to be quite a novelty. I remember jumping onto his lap and due to the fact he had his foot resting on the rung of the chair, my extra weight broke it off completely. I was promptly chastised and there was embarrassment all round. Eventually we both had to go to bed. For some silly reason we could not stop ourselves giggling. My Father scolded us in a rather stern voice, which we heeded with silence.

The following year, we received a letter to say that my Father had passed away at the age of forty four, due to peritonitis. Apparently he had been poorly for sometime and had developed a tuberculosis ulcer, possibly caused from glass-blowing. Eventually the ulcer burst and poison set in. My mother was now a widow, left to cope with life as it was, with two children at home and four evacuated to different parts of the country. Life went on in our village as usual, with the exception of an incendiary bomb dropping in one of the fields, creating a huge crater. This was big news amongst the locals. Then another day a German plane crashed quite nearby, leaving shrapnel scattered on window ledges. A trickle of excitement ran through us. After all, being in the country, these sort of events didn't happen very often.

I had not seen my mother during the five years that I lived in the country and, as far as I was concerned, we were happy to stay with our new family who, after five years, we had grown to love. We were one big happy family, we were surrounded with love and we were content with living in a comfortable environment. This, after all, was the life that I knew and was familiar with. The news that "The War is over!" meant very little to me, why should it, we were all very happy the way things were, what more could we possibly want? Soon the realisation of what this meant started to dawn on me when Mrs Cook said that we would be able to go home soon. I told her that this was my home now,"I'm staying here", I said, "I'm not going back!". After many tantrums and lots of tears, the day came for us to return to God knows where? I will never forget that day! A mixture of tears, stiff upper lip, nausea and reassurances of meeting again overwhelmed us. The feelings were indescribable and the pain of parting had a destructive effect later.

The train chugged into the little peaceful station. Our guardians were there to see us off. We were gently hoisted onto the train. I remember I was holding back the tears because I did not want them to get upset and I guess they were doing the same. After the kisses and fretful goodbyes, the train began to pull out of the station. With our arms extended as far as possible, we waved continuously, until they were mere specks in the distance and then they were gone. I felt such an ache in my heart and I fell into a very numb, hurting silence, full of a very deep sadness at what we had left behind. I cannot remember any of the journey back. I think I must have switched off from things around me in an attempt to suppress the hurt I felt inside.

I have a faint memory of arriving at the very busy, noisy and smokey station of Paddington, of being met by a small lady, with her hair tied back looking rather nervous. "Was this my Mother?" I thought. She greeted me with a kiss. I remember treating this sign of affection with very cool air. We then boarded the underground train, which terrified me. The next thing I remember, was approaching some very tall, dismal looking buildings and then a door being opened by two quizzical young girls. One of them wore metal framed glasses and the other had a very round face, framed by a short fringe. I assumed one was my sister but did not know which. Soon it became clear, that the one who wore spectacles, was my youngest sister, Ann. Being use to the large open spaces made the flats look like a prison. Our three bedroomed house was home to two families. Our family of seven being one family and my aunt, uncle and three cousins being the other. I discovered that I had to sleep with my mother, who although she was my mother was still a stranger to me. I became very resentful towards my mother and the surroundings that I now found myself. I cried every night which, looking back, must have been awful for mother, trying to sleep next to me.

I yearned to go back to 'my home' for some time and eventually I returned for a holiday. The excitement was tremendous. Inevitably, when it was time to return to my real family in London, the same feelings returned. As a consequence of refusing to go back to London, I was able to stay for a further seven months. Eventually I had to leave, despite requests from Mrs Cook to allow her to adopt me. Much to my resentment, my mother turned down these requests. However I was able to return many times to visit my other family in the country. Over the following years I was able to introduce many members of my family and friends to my foster folks. Given the opportunity, I would have visited them more but after each visit there was always the pain of saying goodbye to them.

At fifteen I began working in a little dairy office. It was during this period that I became agoraphobic. I became very insecure and I had panic attacks, which remained with me for many years.

Eventually I married and had four sons. They have all visited my haven in the country. In later years, even my grandchildren were welcomed. Sadly at different times over the following years, Mrs Cook, Mrs Sully and Harry all passed on. These were all very sad and traumatic occasions for me. In spite of all the traumas and sadness I have endured having been evacuated, I would not have missed the love and happiness that those lovely people gave to me. I hope that my experience made me a more understanding and spiritual human being. No one is to blame for what happened. It was just something that happened during a very sad time in history. My Mother is ninety three years of age now and she is quite poorly in hospital. I work as a carer in the same residential home where my mother now lives. Bless her!

Rene and I were remembered in Harry's will for which we were very grateful but we were more grateful for the love and care, that was given to us through those very impressionable years.

•

Dear Alice

Thank you so much for sharing your 'War Time Memories' with us here, it really has been my privilege to be allowed to use your story in my book. Like so many dear evacuees at that time, you did not really know where home was, as you so rightly say, you were loved and were happy, what more can any child want, but to grow up where they are loved and wanted. I can quite understand how you went on to suffer from agoraphobia and panic attacks. Thank God that you came through it all and went on to be a loving and caring person, which I know has a lot to do with Mr and Mrs Sully and Mrs Cook, for the love they showed you when you were so young. Looking back I can see how much your own mother and father must have suffered when they had to part with you and your siblings. I am sure like many at that time they were only thinking of your safety, but we now know they were the ones who lost those very important years of bonding with you.

My thanks and best wishes to you,

Michael

Chapter VII

Moses Luff's Story

I know that many of my older readers, if I may call you that, still treasure the memories they have of their fathers who gave their lives in the Great War of 1914 to 1918. One such gentleman is Les Luff, who has told me how much my book 'My Dad My Hero' moved him. Les, quite rightly, thought of his father as his hero. The following story is our tribute to Moses and may he rest in peace with his many comrades, all of whom gave so much for our today.

Moses was born at Long Sutton, Lincolnshire on 18th February, 1885. He was the youngest of three children, the other two being girls, Florence and Helen. At the age of twenty six he married Miss Ethel Ann Rowton, a local girl, aged 18. His first son, Moses Edward William was born on 5th March, 1914.

In April, 1916, he was called up under National Service and after Induction and Initial Training at Lincoln, he was sent to France. Here he joined 'B' Company, 1st Battalion, Lincolnshire Regiment on 29th May as part of reinforcements to bring back the Battalion to full strength. The Battalion then had approximately 840 to 860 men.

An Infantryman went into war carrying a minimum load of 66lbs. This equipment consisted of the following:
Haversack containing:
Shaving gear, Extra socks, Unconsumed portion of days ration, Special emergency rations, Field dressing and iodine, Steel helmet, Gas helmet and goggles, Rolled ground sheet, Water bottle, Entrenching tool, Mess tin, 2 sandbags, 220 rounds of ammunition, Rifle and bayonet

A soldier was part of an organisation made up of many parts. The Army organisation consisted of:
Section = 12-15 Men plus NCO
4 Sections = 1 Platoon

4 Platoons = 1 Company
4 Companies = 1 Battalion (Approximately1000 men including:
30 Officers, 1 Doctor, 24 Stretcher Bearers,1 Quartermaster, 30
Transport Drivers, Clerks, Cooks, Tailors, Storemen etc)
4 Battalions = 1 Brigade(plus artillery, Ambulance, Signals and
Engineers
3 Brigades =1 Division (Approximately 18073 all ranks)
76 Guns and 24 Machine Guns
3 or 4 Divisions   1 Army Corps

The Battalion was sent to the Somme as part of the 5th
Army, later the 4th, 21st Division and moved into trenches
around Meaulte, south east of Albert.
On the 24th June, a week long bombardment, night and day, on
the German lines, was the prelude to the 1st Battle of the
Somme. The 1st Battalion attacked on the 1st July and during
the first day sustained 110 casualties.
On the 3rd July they sustained a further 234 casualties.
This was his 'blooding' into active service and one cannot
imagine how they coped. The Christmas of 1916 was spent in the
trenches. Following the Somme, Moses served in the Battle of
Arras and Lens near Dainville during 1917. After this battle the
Battalion was withdrawn from the line and put into reserve.
Home leave was granted and some time during July or August
he returned to England for a while. He returned to France for
the Battle of Flanders, Passchendaele and Ypres in October
1917. It rained for days on end, which turned the roads and
fields to a liquid mud. He spoke of wounded soldiers being
sucked down under the mud. When the rains came, the water
drained into the shell craters and, if wounded men were lying in
these craters, they would often drown. It was also very tiring
trying to fight covered in all that mud, struggling to keep your
weapons clean all the time.
On the lighter side of things, I remember him mentioning
that in August, 1916 whilst in trenches at Blagny, the enemy were
only fifteen yards away, separated by rolls of barbed wire. It was
not uncommon for the British troops to lob tins of corned beef
over to the Germans and to receive in return, tins of jam etc!

This could only be done though when the German trenches were occupied by the Saxons, who seemed to be content to 'live and let live'.

In March 1918, he served in the 2nd Battle of the Somme. It was here on the battlefield that he found a silver teaspoon that the family still have today. After this came a period of his war that he always said he would like to forget. This took place on the 16th March when the Battalion was in the line at Bogaert Farm on the Stanyzer Cross Road, east of Kemmel, Wytechaete, which is when the German offensive began.

The German troops came out of rolling fog without any prior artillery fire and over-ran the 1st Battalion. He told me how he tried to find a defending position only to find himself surrounded by German troops. Immediately in front of him, between him and his retreating mates, was a line of German troops, down on one knee, firing at them. His only line of escape was through this line. He ran through the German troops and said he would never forget the sounds of bullets whistling past him as he ran, crying and praying that the Lord would spare him once more, after all he had gone through. His thoughts were on his young wife and son and the new baby due any day. (Neville Victor was born on the 1st May,1918).

As he ran into the fog he saw, more or less straight ahead, a shell hole, which he ran toward. He remembered diving into the hole, head first, thinking that this way at least his head would be out of the line of fire quicker. In the shell hole he found some of his mates and very shortly afterwards, under cover of thickening fog, they managed to move further back and assembled at Seige Farm, north west of Kemmel.

At roll call the Battalion was found to consist of 5 officers and 82 men. 87 men out of a total of over 850 survived. 'B' Company was down to just 17 men out of the original 220. Following this decimation the Battalion was moved south to a so called 'soft' sector to await reinforcements. This proved to be a case of 'out of the frying pan into the fire' as the Battalion, when reinforced, was then involved in the 3rd Battle of the Aisne on 27th May, 1918. During this battle the 1st Battalion was again reduced from around 840 men to 70.

Moses remained an Infantryman for the whole of the time that he was in France and one night he was part of a patrol, out in No-Mans Land, when they were discovered by the Germans. They came under heavy machine gun fire and in the semi-darkness they were unable to find the gap in the wire, through which to return. They decided to crawl their way back under the wire, which with difficulty they did. Only Moses discovered, to his horror, that his rifle must have been pulled from his shoulder as they came through. Looking back he could just about see it in the wire and so he decided to go back for it, even though he was fired upon there and back, he managed to retrieve his rifle. He knew that to return to the Battalion without his rifle could possibly be misconstrued and bring a charge of cowardice, which brought the death sentence.

On another occasion, in the heat of attack and counter-attack, he found himself, late in the day, sheltering in a shell hole close to the enemy trenches. In the same shell-hole, also sheltering, was a German soldier, roughly the same age as himself. After the initial shock, they both accepted each others plight and due to the heavy firing over the shell hole, spent some time together. They exchanged a cigarette and even showed family photographs. When there was lull in the firing they shook hands, said goodbye and went in different directions back to their own lines. They were both fighting a war that neither wanted.

The nearest Moses came to being wounded was on one very cold night, whilst he was on sentry duty in the trenches. He was standing on the firing step facing the enemy and, as the cold was creeping into his feet, he attempted to keep them warm by stamping them. As he stamped his feet his body swayed from side to side. As he was stamping and swaying he became aware of a buzzing sound and then he felt a pain to his left ear lobe. When he was later relieved of duty and checked his ear in a mirror, he discovered that his ear lobe had been shot off by an enemy rifle bullet which came some 1200 yards or so from the enemy trenches. You can see why the infantry were often referred to as the 'PBI' or 'Poor bloody infantry'.

Moses was awarded the Victory Medal and the British War Medal. He had served in the 1st Battle of the Somme, the battle of Arras and Lens, the battle of Flanders, Ypres and Passchendaele. He fought in the 2nd battle of the Somme at Amiens, the battle of Wytechaete at Kemmel, the 3rd battle of the Aisne and at Hill 202 Line of the Vesle.

Following the Armistice, Moses was demobbed at Bachant in 1919 and returned home to see his second son, Neville, for the first time. He was able to return to a so called normal life but fate was to deal him a further blow when, in 1923, his wife died of T.B. at the age of only 30, leaving him with his two young sons aged 9 and 5 years. He brought them up by himself until, in 1929, he met my Mother. I was born in 1931 and my sister Joan, who was to complete his family, was born in 1935. During World War Two Moses served in the Home Guard at Tydd Gote for the Lincolnshire Platoon and was awarded the Defence Medal.

Most of these stories I have discovered through research but some are from snippets of stories I have remembered. Moses was a gentle man who would and did, share his last penny with anyone who was worse off than himself. We all remember him with much love and affection. He died peacefully, aged 86, in 1971 and Mum died two years later. He was my Dad and my best friend.

•

Dear Les,

It has been my privilege to feature your dear late father's story here. I hope it will be a fitting tribute to him. I could not help but be reminded of that old saying "There but for the grace of God go I". We can all imagine how different Moses story would have read if he had not gone back for his rifle. He most likely would have been shot at dawn, like so many other brave shell shocked heroes. We that are left must never forget how much we owe to men like Moses - they have marked the paths of history and I for one hope and pray that mankind will never let such needless deaths of so many young men ever happen again.
Thank you
Michael

Chapter VIII

Bernard Carr's Story

Dear Michael,

Thank you for taking the time to chat with me on the phone the other day and thank you for allowing me to send on my memories to you of my days in World War Two. I have much trouble now with my eyes and cannot see too well these days. I have had to finish driving and my bowling now but worst of all is that I have also had to give up my Magic which, as you know, was my life. My friend has been kind enough to write down my memories, as I have sat and recalled them to mind. I hope that you will be able to use them in your book, it is my story of the part I played for my King and Country.

The following story comes from Bernard Carr, of Crowland, Peterborough. Bernard first made himself known to me many years ago now, after he had read my first book 'My Dad My Hero', to tell me how true it was and how he had also been one of the lucky ones to return home from 'Hell on earth', at the hands of the Japanese, in World War Two. He also went on to tell me that once back into civvy street, he carried on his love of magic, and became a member of the magic circle. When Bernard knew that I was writing this book of 'War Time Memories' he rang me to ask if I would consider using his story. The pleasure is all mine Bernard.

Memories of a Japanese POW

Crowland, the jewel in the South Lincolnshire fens, spawns some of England's most fertile and productive areas of arable land. History has left its mark on this ancient and historic fenland town and its people. Some memories of the second world war are as vivid today as they were back in years 1940 to 45. The years have not dimmed the memories of comrades long gone or the atrocities suffered.

Fate dealt its hand in 1940 when at the age of nineteen, with everything to live for, I was called up. I have been told that I was a happy-go-lucky lad, in and out of various jobs but I had a steady girlfriend, named Ethel, the love of my life! Nothing could prepare me for the events that were to follow.

The country was in turmoil at the outbreak of war and the sons of Crowland were off to fight for their King and Country, with me amongst them. Many of them were never to return home again. As I sat there on the train gazing out on territory that I had never seen before, I reflected on my life so far and wondered what the future held in store for me. If I had known then what was to befall me I would not have been so eager to get on with my training and get this damn war over with.

I had been posted to Blackdown in Dorset to be turned into a soldier. Life had not prepared me for the rigours of Army discipline but I soon learnt to toe the line with plenty of rifle and foot drill, including marching 25 to 50 miles a day in heavy combat gear. We were taught how to load and fire a 3.7 heavy anti-aircraft gun, which could easily burst your ear drums and in many cases often did.

No punches were pulled in training. Life had not prepared me to kill anyone and yet here I was being taught bayonet practice with the emphasis on thrusting the bayonet into the enemies stomach, twisting it and pulling it out and being told in no uncertain terms "well lads if you don't do it to them first, it will be you that's dead, so you'd better wake up and do it". I was learning fast and life would never be the same again. I soon came to the conclusion that we had little chance of actually hitting an enemy plane but we could make them fly higher to avoid our flack, this made it much harder for them to carry out accurate bombing. I often think of those young R.A.F pilots who were only as old as myself but who took on the German Airforce, we had very few planes but still those brave lads beat them off and stopped Germany from invading our dear Great Britain. I cannot praise the R.A.F. enough. After training I was posted to the 77th Welsh Regiment 241 Battery Heavy Anti Aircraft Royal Artillery stationed at Leeds, followed by Nantwich, Bude in Cornwall, Penalan in Cardiff and Merry Hill Barracks, in Glasgow.

At the end of my training I set sail from Grenoch, on the 'Empress of Australia' to cape Town, South Africa and saw Table Mountain whilst on shore leave, it really was very beautiful. I then rejoined the ship and set sail for Java, Dutch Indies in the far east, these were only places that I had read about but little did I know what was in store for me, alas I was soon to find out! When we arrived in Java, we were put on a train that was to take us to our gun sight in Sourebaya but the train was sabotaged and sadly we ran head on into a train coming in the opposite direction. Our train telescoped and a lot of our chaps were killed or very badly injured. The injured and dying were taken to a local hospital and we heard later that when the Japs landed that many of these lads, along with the doctors and nurses from the hospital, were bayoneted to death. Many of them were also beheaded. The local people of men, women and children, were gunned down as they were forced into the sea. We later saw hundreds of bodies floating in the sea and the waves were red with blood.

A few days later we travelled by road to our gun sight in Sourebaya - we had four anti-aircraft guns which we manned there. We never saw any British, Dutch, or Malay planes, only Japanese, they came over at will in formations of 27. We knew after a week or two that we were losing the battle. We had now run out of ammunition for our guns. We were told by our officers that it was now every man for himself, yet 52 of us were ordered to stay behind and destroy the guns so that the Japs could never use them. Once we had done this we found a boat and escaped to a small island called Maderia, eventually we had to come back to the mainland because the Japs threatened to bomb the island if we did not give ourselves up to them. So we returned to Batavia, to become prisoners. On the way we saw many heads stuck on poles, this was done to show us all, including the civilians, what would happen to us if we did not obey all Japanese orders.

When we arrived at Batavia, we were kicked and hit with rifle butts before being marched off to a prison camp. Each day we worked on the docks clearing up bomb damage and every day someone was beaten up or killed by the guards, one just had to hope and pray it was not you that they picked on. After months of being moved from camp to camp we were eventually put on a ship, which was loaded with bombs and shells. We journeyed hundreds of miles to our next prison camp, which was on the island called Huroku, our task now was to build an airstrip for the Japs. This place turned out to be a living hell for us for once again. Each day we were beaten and kicked by the hateful guards, many times we were beaten with rifle butts and the really unlucky ones were beheaded, because they could not work fast enough. The rest of us would be made to line up and watch these dear comrades meet their horrific death, looking back it really was the only escape from hell on earth at that time. One of the reasons we could not work was because we were starving, I myself went down to just under six stone. In time the Japs, learnt that if they killed every man that could not keep up with the work, then they would have to kill us all, then who would do their work for them. This did not stop them amusing themselves with punishment to us though. Those who could not work were put into what was known as pig baskets. In these you could not move, there was only room to kneel in them, they were placed in the open so that you suffered in the full heat of the day and felt the bitter cold throughout the night. You passed your bodily motions where you knelt, you were covered in sores, maggots and flies. There was no food or water given to you and the Jap guards would take great delight in prodding you in the eyes with a bamboo stick. The Japs enjoyed doing this, there was no reason for it, it was just done for their own amusement, the only escape, as I said, was death. When we arrived at this camp there were 2,075 men but only 750 of us were left alive when it came time to move back to Java. I really was one of the lucky ones.

Life went on much the same for us as we were only needed to work on building the Japs railway, or airfields. Early each morning at 7am we marched off to work and returned at 9-30pm that evening. The first thing we did was bury our dead, before we were given our daily cup of rice. Sleep was almost impossible due to the conditions we had to live under, such as leaking roofs, the cold of night, the bugs, sheer exhaustion and illness, yes unconsciousness was a happy release. In the wet season the roof leaked and we just lay on the floor in the mud and wet, we did not have the luxury of a bed. Things were really getting worse for us as time went on and when we were moved to Ambon, I became very ill, so ill that I could not work. I just lay in the hut but of course if you did not work you did not receive your rice, only a cup of rice water. I was saved by two R.A.F chaps who used to crawl under the wire fence at night and raid the Japanese bins for scraps of food. If it had not been for them I know that I would not be here today to recall my memories. One of these brave lads was called Fred Lenton, from Long Sutton and the other was Reg Constable, from Black Drove, Thorney. Both of these dear lads died in Ambon. It was such a shame because out of the three of us, I should have been the one that did not make it home, because they were still working and going out on work parties each day. It was not to be for them though but once I arrived home and was well enough to visit people I used to call on Reg Constables mother and take her a box of chocolates. It was not until after her death that I found out that she had been a diabetic and could not eat them but she never ever told me this for fear of upsetting me. At least I had the privilege to tell her what a great son her Reg had been and of how he saved my life.

I can recall the three hateful guards, we nicknamed 'Freeman, Hardy & Willis', who would come into our huts at night drunk and kick and beat us up, I know that they really enjoyed doing this. I remember once carrying a chap's coffin, for he had died of Berri-berrie which meant that he was full of water, well the poor chap literally burst whilst we were carrying him, of course we got soaked as it poured out of his coffin.

We were on a starvation diet and had to supplement our half cup of rice with whatever we could with things such as frogs, dogs, cats, snakes, snails,and sometimes bits of buffalo, in fact anything that moved we considered eating, if we could catch it.

I still recall how our doctors were having to amputate legs from our boys, that were full of ulcers, all this was done without anaesthetic. To try and save a leg they were scooping out ulcers with a spoon, because they had no other medical supplies available. One never forgets the screams of pain that these dear lads gave out during this treatment. Most of us lost at least half our body weight while prisoners and suffered exhaustion, Dysentry, Malaria, Berri-berrie, Palegrin and of course, starvation. You could visit our so called toilets at least 20 times a day when suffering from dysentry, which made you very weak and of course, many times you never even made it to the latrines. The worst thing was that you had to pass the Japanese guards and go through the formality of bowing to them. If you did not do this you were beaten by the guards at once, so of course, many times you messed yourself, which the jap guards took great delight in laughing at. I must mention for the world to know, that the Japs massacred 312 Australians on the island of Ambon. Some were shot and some beheaded. This massacre took place on a coconut plantation, after they had fought off the Japs for two months, even though they were heavily out numbered, they really were such brave lads. It was also reported in a New Zealand newspaper called 'Windmill Post' that sixty witnesses saw a number of British and other P.O.W's put into pig baskets, then taken out to sea and thrown over the side of the ship to feed the sharks. I was reminded by an ex-prisoner only recently of another occasion when one of our comrades was buried up to his neck for some trivial offence and left for three days and nights, his tongue and face became incredibly swollen from the heat of the day and from every Jap guard kicking his head every time they passed him. He was given no food or water, so our padre tried to intervene by giving him a drink of water but of course he too was badly beaten for his efforts. I cannot recall which service this poor prisoner had been in, but he eventually died. I know that his regiment lost another brave soul that day. I still cannot understand how any race can treat other human beings in this way.

Those of us still left alive were shipped back to Singapore. During the journey we were to witness the murder of an R.A.F. corporal named Taylor. He was seen stealing some dried fish, by a Jap guard. He was taken to a real bastard of a Jap officer, who we called 'Yellow Boots'. Corporal Taylor had got rid of the dried fish before coming in front of Yellow boots but Yellow boots at once set about beating him for quite some time - there was nothing we could do to help him. Yellow boots also held a revolver to the lower part of Corporal Taylors body but still Taylor, refused to admit that he had stolen the dried fish. As Yellow boots shouted out "my guards not lie to me", he tied a rope under Taylors armpits and lowered him over the side of the ship, indicating that if he did not confess he would become shark bait. We all shouted at him to confess and eventually he did. Corporal Taylor, was hauled back on board ship and Yellow boots let him go, as he had won the day and had not lost face in front of his Japanese troops, who were all enjoying seeing Taylor suffering. At our next port of call Yellow boots went ashore for six hours shore leave. Those P.O.W's, including Corporal Taylor, suffering from dysentry, were queuing up to do their business over the side of the ship. The Japanese captain of the ship beckoned Taylor to take his turn over the side, when Taylor stepped forward he was seen by the same Jap guard that had reported him over the dried fish incident. When Yellow boots, returned to the ship, he was very drunk, so the guard reported Taylor to him again. Yellow boots sent for Taylor to be brought before him again. He at once set about beating Taylor, who was pleading for him to stop but the Jap officer showed no mercy and Corporal Taylor died that day on the deck of the ship after being kicked to death. Nearly every bone in his body was broken and you could not recognise his face at all. His body was put in an old sack and thrown overboard. We all stood to attention as this was done. Our thoughts were with poor Taylor, everyone was so quiet, as they thought of what they could have done to save him. Two British officers and a Sgt. Major Harvoed, were called before Yellow boots. Because they protested so much, he at once started beating the officers. The Sgt. Major was made to stand to attention and Yellow boots hit him over the head with a bottle, he then picked up a second bottle and hit him over the head again splitting his head wide open. The bottle contained a type of disinfectant which ran into the Sgt. Majors, eyes and of course his head wound, we could all see that it was causing him a lot of pain. Yellow boots then picked up a third bottle, at which point the Sgt. Major made a run for it with Yellow boots in hot pursuit.

We shouted to the ships officers to please stop Yellow boots but no one intervened until a Japanese soldier beckoned the Sgt.Major up to the top deck and quickly pushed him into a doorway, which he then stood in front of. Yellow boots ran straight past him but thankfully at last the ship's captain intervened and ordered Yellow boots to go below to his cabin and sleep off the drink. However, before doing this Yellow boots made his way back to the top deck, he had the two officers stand to attention on the deck below him, while he urinated on them from above. The two officers remained at attention with great dignity, while Yellow boots carried out this disgraceful act. When we finally docked at Singapore I am not too sure what happened, for as soon as the gang plank was lowered Yellow boots was taken off to be met by a little Japanese man wearing silly little short pants, suspenders and white socks. He wore a large sword that was much to big for him but he took Yellow boots off to the Kempei-Tai, who were the main Japanese police. They arrested Yellow boots but of course I don't know if he ever received any punishment for the deaths and suffering that we had received from him. I feel sure that it must have been due to the disdain of the ships captain, that Yellow boots was arrested.

On one occasion, before going on a work party, I decided to wrap my cup of rice in some leaves and hide it in the fork of a tree to save it for my dinner, when I returned I was very hungry and went to retrieve my ration of rice. When I unwrapped it, it was sour and covered in ants but I was so hungry that I hate it all including the ants. My pal said it was the most vitamins I'd had for years. Later I noticed that our Jap guard had not eaten all his rice so I said to my pal that I was going to ask him if I could have it. I could speak a little Japanese and Malay by now, so I went up to the guard and bowed to him four or five times, giving him plenty of bull shit and said "Sia mow banyaknazi goring" which should have said "could I have a little more of your fried rice" but what I actually said was "could I have a lot more fried rice" I found out later that what I should have used was the word "Sidcut" which means little and sadly I had used the word "Banyak" which means a lot. The guard gave me a good beating instead, with the butt of his rifle. I was so lucky that it was time for us all to start work, as I feel sure that if it had not been then he would have finished me off. When he stopped beating me he tipped his rice out on the ground beside me and rubbed it into the ground with his boot.

I was finally repatriated from Singapore, from a camp called River Valley. We were saved by the Atom Bomb, I say god bless the pilot that flew that plane, for he saved thousands like me, as well as the civilian population, who at the time were still being murdered by the Japs. We knew that we were going to be machine gunned if any Allied Forces had landed on the island. All prisoners were to be disposed of, under orders from Tokyo.

I came home on the 'Almonsora'. My girlfriend, Ethel, had waited over three and a half years for me, this meant so much to me because a lot of my comrades who were married came home to find that their wives had run off with someone else. I am sorry to say that I don't think that I was worth waiting for, because most Jap P.OW's do not make the best husbands, as they think a lot about the past and even today we still find it difficult to get the images of all the beatings and beheadings, which we were forced to watch, out of our heads. We of course, still have the memories of our comrades, whom we left behind in some horrible jungle grave, having died from the beatings, disease and starvation. Even if we can put it all out of our minds in the day, it always seems to come back to haunt us at night in our dreams.

I would like to put on record, that the Crowland council can be proud of what they did for all those that had been involved in the war effort and to finish on a happy note by stating that I married my girlfriend, Ethel, after the war and we celebrated our Golden wedding Anniversary in 1995.

Over the last few years I have endeavoured to track down some of those old army mates who were prisoners of war with me but alas I find that there are not many of us left alive now. Some years ago I went to one of our FEPOW reunions, I was telling another FEPOW about the murder of Corporal Taylor, on the Jap ship whilst we were being transported to Singapore. He listened intently and then said, "Stay here, I want you to meet someone". He returned a few minutes later with an ex R.A.F.

chap named Ray Healey, who had told him the very same story. Yes, it turned out that Ray and myself had both witnessed the murder of Corporal Taylor, needless to say we had a long chat into the 'wee' small hours of the next morning about our dreadful experience at the hands of those hateful Japanese during World War Two. Ray is now 81 years old and we still chat on the phone together about those far off days but in our minds it all seems like yesterday. We will never forget our dear comrades though, for they died from such brutal treatment, all for King and Country and to give us our lives today. May they rest in Peace.

●

Dear Bernard

Thank you for sharing your War Time Memories with us, my readers that have read my first three books will know already just what special men all FEPOW's are. I know that so many of them ask me "when will you do another book of true stories about these great men?". I feel sure that they will have found your story of great interest, for I find that when I write up a FEPOW's story, even though you were all treated so horrifically by your hateful captors, that each one of you has a different story to tell. As you know my late father, who was one of your comrades, always said to me "remember Michael, there but for the grace of God go I". How true this saying is, for as you will know only too well, things can change very quickly, none more than when in the grips of a World War. I know that as long as you live, you will never forget your dear comrades Fred Lenton and Reg Constable, who gave so much, to give you your today. Destiny had other plans for you Bernard and as you so rightly say you were one of the lucky ones. Those that know you as a Magical Entertainer, who brings such pleasure to all his audiences, will now know that you yourself found that Magic needed to get you through that hell on earth, that you were thrown into in World War Two. We thank you for what you gave and suffered for our today.

Yours most sincerely,
Michael.

Chapter IX

Joanne Walker's Story

The following short story comes from Mrs Joanne Walker, of Newmarket, Suffolk. Joanne, first heard me on BBC Radio Cambridgeshire, doing my War Time Memories programme, with that lovely presenter Mandy Morton. Many of you will remember that it was Mandy that inspired me to write my book 'War Time Women' and I can't thank her enough for that, for it has helped raise thousands of pounds for Breast Cancer Research. Joanne first made herself known to me when I gave a talk to Newmarket Townswomen's Guild. We then met again when I was the after dinner speaker for the Newmarket Horticulture Club. This time we had an opportunity to chat together over our meal and Joanne, told me how much enjoyment she received from my war time memories programmes with the BBC.

I told her how she may find it of interest to write down some of her own war time memories and allow me have a read of them, about a year later I received the following story.

War Time Rent Collector

The day war broke out, I recall the general thoughts of the country were, "It will never be the same again" How true those thoughts were. Only 21 years earlier we had seen the war to end all wars, yet here was mankind ready to start all over again. As you say Michael, will mankind ever learn?

On that fateful day of 3rd September 1939, when war was declared, I was 24 years old, with a 4 year old daughter to care for. My husband who was in the airforce, would now be away from us and would find himself in all kinds of danger. My parents lived nearby to me and thankfully were always delighted to look after my little girl, Sheila. I could have been exempt from work with the war effort, as I had a child but as I was able to arrange such good care for her, I was only too glad to be able to offer my services, even in a simple way. I knew I could definitely not consider the services as I needed to be there for Sheila and keep the family home going for when my husband came home on leave.

Before my marriage I had worked for an estate agents and in our local paper I saw an advert for a rent collector. I had never done anything like it before but I thought that it would be an interesting job, with the chance to be out and about. As the office was near to where I lived, I applied for it, I remember I put my age as 26, as I thought it seemed a more responsible age for this sort of position. I was successful and was given the job, which entailed covering a large area of the western side of London, such as Nottinghill, Ladbrook Grove, Harrow Road, Harlesdon, Kensington, Portobello Road, Paddington, Maida Vale, Hampstead, Kilburn, etc. I should mention that my job was a reserved occupation, as I took it over from a man, who was fit and healthy and of the right age to be called up to fight for his country. I just hope that he came through it all okay.

I lived on the outskirts of London and so a fairly safe area when it came to enemy action. My job did entail daily travelling on various bus routes into London. This meant travelling in many parts where bombing was inevitable and of course miles of walking the streets. The properties varied from large houses, many storied types, with 'Upstairs Downstairs' residences and of course the basement dwellers and the little back to back rows of houses. As you can imagine this also meant I had many steps to climb during my day's work. Many of the properties also had stables. Others were what we called 'two up and two down' houses with the front room door opening straight onto the road.

It was quite usual in those days to see horse drawn carts all over the place, many would be Rag and Bone men and these people ran yards in which their home and stable would be. When I went to many of these stables to collect rent, I had to search and fumble, amongst sacks of rags, to find the rent books. I would have been told where to look for these rent books but I feel sure some just wanted to have a game with me and set me a merry task to try and find them. Years later when I watched Steptoe and Son on television, I could have sworn that they were using some of the establishments that I had collected from all those years before. Many of the house's were already in run down areas and of course, many had no hot water. Even the large five floor houses would only have the one toilet, that all the residents would have had to share. Times were hard, even without the worry of war and the bombing raids from Hitlers henchmen.

The rents ranged from four shillings and twopence, to twelve shillings and eightpence, a week. In the very poor areas the tenants were always so very kind and thoughtful, as I reached the door to their property it would open and a welcoming voice would say "come in dear" and take a seat by the fire and warm yourself. The winters were so cold in those days, that of course this kindness was always much appreciated, thankfully the summers were very hot, not like the mixture we get today.

Once in and seated the tenant would lift the chenille table cloth and there under it would be the rent books laid out, for every room in the house. All the money would be just right, no change needed to be given. This really was such a great help, as there was no waiting about, no stairs to climb and I always received such a kind welcome. These dear, poor, everyday people really were the backbone of our great country. In winter they always offered me a hot drink and in summer a cold drink, these people were so very different from the, supposable, better class of person in their large grand properties.

I well recall one cold winters day, when I called at one of these grand houses. I knocked on the door and, after what seemed like ages, the lady tenant answered the door and said "Oh! Has the week come round already? It comes round far too quickly don't you know" She then said "You wait there while I go and fetch your rent money, as I don't want to let the cold into the house", with this the door was slammed shut in my face. After a while she came back with the rent, which I took and marked off in her rent book, then without a bye-your-leave the door was shut in my face again. As you can see, very different from the poor working class families, who were so kind and willing to share what little they had with you.

As you can imagine, I walked so many miles in this job that my footware soon wore out and what with rationing it was hard to replace them. I can assure you that I knew all about putting cardboard and paper inside my shoes to cover the holes in the worn out soles.

Many times as I walked the streets collecting the rents, the deafening sound of the air raid sirens would scream out, especially during the blitz. Frequently at such times a nearby door would open and someone would pull me inside. I would find myself huddled under a table, or in some shelter, with complete strangers, clutching their hands and holding our breath as the bombs whistled down on us. Later in the war when the 'Doodle Bugs', V1 or V2 rockets came, we would wait for the thud and explosion. Although it was terrifying, to realise that some poor souls nearby had received a tragic disaster, I think most of us thanked God that we had been spared and of course, we were always so pleased to hear the all clear siren. I will never forget the wonderful companionship and christianity, of those days, offered to me by total strangers. These dear people taught me so much.

Because things were on ration, you had to scrimp and save all you could just to make ends meet. One day one of my dear old tenants was putting up a stiff black netting onto her windows, one side of this was sticky and stuck to the glass window panes, this we used to help stop the glass splintering and flying into the room during an air raid. This material was ration free, so you did not have to use your coupons to get it. The dear old lady told me that if you soaked the material in water for a few hours, that it went really soft and was good for making clothes. As my husband was coming home on leave I thought I would give it a try for myself. I obtained some of this netting material and, after giving it a good soak, I made a lovely black net nightie, I sowed some yellow ribbons on the shoulders and had myself a nice new nightie. When my husband saw it he said "That looks nice darling, how many coupons did that take". I think he laughed when I told him what I had done and just said "Don't forget to thank the dear old lady for telling you about it, you look really nice in it". My husband's 48 hour leave was soon gone and he was off again and for me it was back to the every day struggle.

One day I stopped at a shelter for my one penny cup of tea, although I was running late I was tempted to stay for another. I then had to run to catch the trolley bus which was just leaving the stop. I did manage to touch it but could just not get on, "Oh dear", I thought to myself, now I really am late. A minute later I heard a terrific bang, alas the bus had been hit by a bomb and most of those on board were killed or badly maimed. I had not even realised that there had been an air raid warning and so I stood with my feet firmly on the ground waiting for the next trolley bus to come along. When there was a raid on we had been warned that if we had to remain standing we were to stand on tip-toe so that the shock waves coming from any bomb blasts would run through our bodies better. As I said I had mine firmly on the ground and received some spinal damage from the blast and, although I managed to get home, I had to then be taken to hospital for treatment. I was also instructed that when there was fear of an imminent bombing raid that if there was nowhere to shelter one must lay flat on the pavement. This I must admit I had to do many times, my boss always said, "Do be careful when you lay down dear, to have the rent money well underneath you and keep it safe." A typical boss, no mention of my safety, only worried about his money.

Many times when I did reach my area to collect the rents, I would find signs up saying "Diversion", "Beware of falling masonry", "Road Closed" or "Holes in Road" etc. There were even times when the houses that I had to collect from were badly damaged or even demolished. On one occasion I arrived at a house and the lady opened the door to me, I could see at once that there was nothing of the house left, just the front wall left standing. She stood amongst the rubble of what had once been her home, she said "I don't think that there is anything left to pay rent on my dear." I expressed my concern to her and left her to try and find what belongings she could amongst the rubble. As I arrived at my next call once again the lady who opened the door, asked me if I would come in and see her husband, I thought "Oh no not another disaster" but on entering the room I noticed a coffin laying on the dinning room table. The lid of the coffin stood in the corner of the room, so of course the coffin was open and laying there inside it was her dead husband. She said "I knew that you would want to pay your last respects to him, so I will leave you with him for awhile." I don't think I was really frightened, because he looked so peaceful but I know I thought to myself of how no one would believe the things one sees as a rent collector.

One day a sweet little old lady who lived in a very run down area opened her door to me, she looked so dirty and unwashed. She had a big saftey pin holding her cardigan together, where most ladies would have worn a brooch. As she opened the door to me the smell hit me at once and I felt quite sick. She said "Oh! you do smell nice my dear" I had no perfume on, for what little perfume I had I kept for very special occasions such as when my husband came home on leave. I think that the poor lady smelt so bad herself that just the smell of me, smelt good to her.

While walking the streets collecting rents, I did also see many pleasant things like the man with his Barrel Organ, what a delightful sound it made and one day I even had the thrill of being given the opportunity to turn the handle. I heard some onlookers say "I think that has been a life long ambition of her's, she looks like she's enjoying it so much." How right they were for it was times like these that never leave your memory. When all around us the world was going mad, we were still all singing on a little back street corner in London.

My boss, who was also a Baptist Minister, would not let me wear slacks in spite of the bitter cold and all the hanging around I did waiting for buses. He said "It's not at all lady like to wear slacks", When I think of the times I had to lay on the pavement wearing a skirt, I now know why so many men smiled at me so often. As I told my boss, I was doing a man's job really and they would all have been wearing trousers but it did no good with his old fashioned Victorian attitude.

One day, due to road closures following the bombings, I was advised to travel home by tube train. I took this advice and this turned out to be another one of those war time experiences that I will never forget. Due to the bombings there was so much havoc above ground that day, that the tube trains were also disrupted. We had to make lots of stops in many strange places. At one station, which I believe was Charing Cross, we came to a stop and I was told that it would be better for me to stay here for the night. This I did and found myself with hundreds of other people doing the same thing. Of course many of these people spent all of the war years sleeping like this, night after night in their own pitches. They had built bunk beds up against the walls, which were several decks high. They had their own cooking appliances and seemed happy to be amongst their own tube mates, ready for another enjoyable evening of singing, before settling down for a nights sleep. Outside, above ground, the blitz was going on and many of them said "I wonder if we shall have homes to go back to in the morning". I was very lucky as I had a seat to rest on, others just slept on the station platform. In the morning a family of total strangers cooked breakfast and shared what they had with me. Such kindness and togetherness surely got us all through those dark days.

I also recall a day when in one area I was trying to collect the rent but none of the tenants seemed to be in. This started to worry me when suddenly from a nearby house someone shouted from a bedroom window "You won't collect any rent from round here for awhile love! They've all gone 'opping". This puzzled me as I thought he meant that they had all done a moonlight flit, which was the saying if anyone had cleared out of the house during the night without paying the rent. Someone then explained to me that they had all gone hop picking in Kent, where they could earn very good money. So from then on at this time of year, I was prepared for dozens of tenants to go missing for several weeks at a time as they went off on their annual hop picking work. When they returned, every penny of the owing rent was always paid in full.

Many of the properties that my employers looked after were owned by people away in the armed forces. The salvage people, of course, had to deal with bombed premises and they would remove all solid items left intact. These would include fire places, WC's, baths, sinks, wash basins, etc. They removed them from the properties and stored them in a large park and as one of my bus rides took me by this park I saw row upon row of these items getting longer by the day. This also highlighted just how bad things were and of course how many homes we were losing.

My parents home suffered badly from bomb damage and on one occasion was left in a terrible mess. My daughter, who would have been about 6 years old at the time, said "Oh dear Grandma, the war has demolished your spring cleaning". It is incredible that even in times of danger children, with their innocence, can bring one such joy.

I recall one very terrifying experience when fire bombs were dropped in a built up area where I was collecting rent. Everyone had to just dash and rush away from their homes. These house's were built right onto the pavement, which meant the front door opened out onto the street. As I rushed by these house's, running and looking for somewhere to shelter, I could see the people inside them grabbing what possessions they could carry, knowing that this would probably be the last time they saw their homes in one piece. Many of these house's were already well alight as those dear people tried to save something to help them through those hard times. Looking back, I know that I was one of the lucky ones to come through World War Two. There were many times when I was very near to death, huddled under someone's table or crouched in a corner of their shelter.

As I look back now my memories of that time seem like it happened only yesterday. At 86 years young, I have many happy memories of those times in my life. Before I took on the job of a rent collector, the Portobello Road was unknown to me but since then it has remained very close to my heart. It is a very long road, from Harrow Road to Nottinghill. It is the Nottinghill end that is famous for it's market at weekends. In the war I was only in this area on weekdays but even then many people had stalls outside their houses on which they would sell things. If you wished to buy anything you just knocked on the door, or called out through the open door, for the occupier to come and serve you. I brought many things at this time from stalls such as these and still treasure them to this day. One is a large antique brass candle stick that I brought for 6d. I always say to people that I was lucky because I found Portobello Road before the Americans did. I am still very sentimental about all the hours I spent there and I often buy friends and family souvenirs with

Portobello Road written on them, such as mugs and plates etc. I also have a name sign some two feet long with Portobello Road printed on it. When I, myself, have a stall for charity events, I always take my sign to hang up over my stall and I am always pleased to hear all the charming people say, "Oh look it's the lady with her Portobello Road stall.

Thank you for asking me to recall my memories of World War Two, I hope that they have been of help and interest to you.

•

Thank you Joanne, for taking my advice in sharing some of your War Time Memories with me and for allowing me to share them with my readers. I feel sure that so many of them that are near to your age, will recall many of the things you mention. I wonder how long the black nightie lasted. I laughed to myself when writing up how the dear old lady asked you in to to see her husband. I dare say it was quite a shock for you when you spotted the coffin on the table. It's always so good to hear of the friendship and comradeship that everyone shared in those dark days. As I have mentioned before in my books, if we could have that same spirit today things would be much better for us all. I look forward to meeting you again when I return to Newmarket to give one of my war time talks.
God Bless and keep you,
Michael

Chapter X

Joan Walton's Story

The following story comes from Mrs Joan Walton, of Oakham, Leicestershire. Joan first heard me a few years ago doing a War Time Memories programme with BBC Radio Leicestershire, with that great presenter, John Florance. Thankfully Joan was inspired to put pen to paper and forward her war time memories on to me in 1998. I had originally hoped to use Joan's story in my book 'Waving Goodbye' but realised that it did not feature well with the stories of evacuees. I kept it on file and once I started writing this book, I knew that there was a place for it. I rang Joan who, I think, had given up on me and I asked her if she remembered sending her story to me in 1998. I don't think I will ever forget her reply, "Oh yes I do! You are that lovely man I heard on BBC Radio Leicester in 1998. I think I sent you a little about my days in World War Two." I told her that she was right and asked if she would still like to feature in one of my books. She excitedly replied "Oh yes please, this really has made my day, I thought that you did not like my story and had put it in the bin." I hope that you will see, as I did, the important part she and her comrades played by keeping up morale during World War Two. The following is Joan's story.

V.E.S.

Has anybody heard of V.E.S.? Come to think of it did anybody need to hear of V.E.S.? Of course not. We heard plenty of stories about E.N.S.A. and the famous stars who entertained the troops. This was mostly overseas and of course they were doing a very good job but these were professional entertainers. V.E.S. (Voluntary Entertainment Service) was quite different, for we were volunteers, doing a full time job during the day and a troop show most evenings.

I was born in 1926 and lived in Sheffield. When World War II came upon us I was almost 13 years old. Just before war was declared, on 3rd September 1939, I had been evacuated to Loughborough. However, after hearing that war had been declared, I felt increasingly unhappy living with strangers and being away from my home and loved ones. My father, whether he was right or wrong, decided the family should remain together. So when my mother came to visit me for my 13th birthday, she took me home with her. I could not have wished for a better 13th birthday present and looking back it turned out lucky 13 for me. I did miss the luxury though of my weekly sixpenny postal order, sent to me by my favourite uncle, Bob. As many older readers will know sixpence, or a tanner, as we called it, bought you so much in those days. I would spend 2d of it on a ticket for the saturday matinee at the cinema. Another 2d of it on a Mars Bar or Crunchie and the last 2d was to buy treats for the rest of the week. However it was worth the forfeit of sixpence, to be back home with my loved ones.

Many good people of Sheffield will remember the Blitz and of how children had to grow up far to quickly, in this now hurtful world, for ones so young. I became 14 years old and found myself leaving school and starting work, thanks to my family and friends, I also joined V.E.S. to do my bit for King and Country. All the performances that we gave were within a 40 mile radius of the city centre.

There was never time to go home from work, so each group of performers would meet outside the town hall, where we were picked up by a corporation bus, which would take us to our show venue. Also meeting us would be our mums, bringing our freshly ironed costumes and a packed meal, to be eaten while travelling on the bus. Occasionally I was allowed to use my ration book to have a quick meal in the nearby Civic Restaurant, I felt very posh. I was only 14 years old, so this was really something for me to enjoy.

There were several groups of entertainers in V.E.S, each known by its title and best described as a Concert Party. There were the 'Laughter Makers', 'Merry Makers' and 'Comic Capers' but we had the grand title of 'Steel City Stars' - so appropriate for Sheffield. There was a wide range of talent. Most groups would consist of dancers and singers, usually a soprano and tenor, musicians and maybe a 'speciality act'. 'Steel Cities' offered a very varied programme.

I, along with Jean, Dorothy and Eileen, formed a dance group, calling ourselves 'The Four Starlets'. We were led by our dancing teacher, Peggy, a very, very, talented soubrette, who was responsible for all our routines. I suppose our costumes were quite prim, although our pleated tap skirts, were a little above the knee. We performed, I recall, a wonderful Russian dance, led by Peggy. I particularly enjoyed a 'Musical Comedy' routine to the theme of 'All the things you are' in which we wore black market, yellow georgette gowns, which made us feel so elegant. We sported a black velvet orchid in our hair. Often we had to depend on wearing outfits which were made from blackout material.

My sister, Edie and her partner, George, were wonderful accordionists and, apart from the classics, would lead the audiences in community singing. One of the most popular numbers in their repertoire was 'In a monastery Garden', played on a darkened stage, with coloured lights, working off a battery inside the accordion grid. The Soprano, in spotlight, would sing the beautiful words and it was all very effective. George was also an amazing pianist. The troops loved it and the atmosphere was just electric. We had a comedian, ventriloquist and tenor, who also sang duets and Jimmy, a guitarist, who sadly later lost his life in the RAF. There was also Dennis who was a cartoonist and quite an unusual act. Then there was a teenage Xylophonist and 'Dalmo' the magician, complete with top hat, red satin lined cloak and of course his magic wand. On one hair-raising occasion, when I was his assistant during the famous guillotine trick, I found myself replacing the decapitated carrot. After a deathly silence and the curtains, two old army blankets, closing, I discovered that the sharp blade had not been strapped safely and the machine had to be dismantled with me still kneeling down and my head still in place! Never again! One lucky escape was enough for me.

The show was produced by my uncle who always looked immaculate in his evening suit. Of course, there were occasions when in the middle of a show, the sirens would sound and the audience would suddenly vanish!

We often used to arrive home very late, as we travelled by bus. When we arrived home depended on which route the bus took and how many diversions, due to the air raids, that it had to take. At least the journey home gave us time to remove our make up and put our hair in curlers. Getting up for work the following morning was always an effort and I dread to think how often I missed my train to the office in nearby Rotherham. I must mention that my weekly train ticket cost all of 2/6d or half a crown.

We continued to do our troop shows long after the war had finished. In fact they continued until 'Demob' was all but complete. I still treasure my V.E.S. badge, depicting a white Yorkshire Rose. I must share with you the occasion in late 1940, when one evening we were due to give a charity performance at a community centre, just on the edge of the City. The only way to travel was by public transport, which meant it was quite hard work for Edie to carry her accordion to the bus stop and then lift it on and off the bus. I wasn't much help because I had the case of costumes to struggle with. This particular night the air raid started even before we had reached our venue, so we went straight into the air raid shelter, which quickly filled up with the people that were to be our audience. We spent the night dancing, singing and playing music etc. We were all aware of the bombing taking place and so we all sang louder in an effort to keep everyone calm. When the all clear eventually sounded we hauled ourselves from the shelter to see the sky red with the flames which engulfed Sheffield that night. Getting back home was so horrendous and frightening. What would we find? What had happened to our parents? Had we even got a home to go to? We walked for miles, long into the night, before being picked up by a bus but we were dropped off again when the flames wouldn't allow the driver to go any further. My sister and I didn't know what to expect. We were so tired and scared and when we reached what had been the bus station, every bus was either burnt out or still blazing. We did not have much further to go, which was a good job really, because we were still dragging that wretched accordion and it was far too expensive to discard, when on the last stretch of road we fell into a crater and thought we had met our end. Thankfully our dad was soon there to help us and his first words on seeing us were "Your mum's safe" Oh what joy to hear those words. He told us of how he had passed our front door, on his way to find us and we laughed together about it, because the door had been blown some distance from where our house had stood. What I hadn't realised, of course, was that my parents did not know if anything had happened to us, their children. Most of the houses in our area had been razed to the ground. Roads were completely wiped out and later I discovered how many friends of ours had perished. As a result of the Sheffield Blitz we had to live with relatives until we could be re-housed. We were clothed by the Red Cross but at least we were alive.

Unlike so many families, we had come through the nightmare of a World War and had lived to tell the tale. Thank you for allowing me to share my memories of that time in my life and telling of the important work that the members of V.E.S. did to lift the spirits of folks here in England during the war. Perhaps from this you will understand why I feel so strongly about V.E.S. and the part we played in the war, even if in many walks of life we remain unheard of. I was pleased to serve our country, with these wonderful entertainers, even if I was not very old, as some would say "no more than a child". I am now 75 years young and still involved in entertainment and recently choreographed 42nd Street, for our local Operatic Society. So as you can see, I am still enjoying it.

●

Dear Joan,
It has been my pleasure to feature your story. I found it of great interest and can just imagine the enjoyment that you and your troop brought to so many dear people during a time when they feared for their lives. As you will know many of my readers are people that gave so much for King and Country in World War Two. I feel sure they will have happy memories of shows such as yours. I know that Andrea Hoyland will find your story of great interest, for like me, she may be wondering if her late mother, Doris Howard, might have once been your bus conductress. Anyone who has read 'War Time Women' will at once recall the story of Doris and her adventures on the Sheffield buses. Long may you be able to keep up the good work that you and your friends do in bringing enjoyment to others, for I can see that it really is in your blood.
Yours thankfully,
Michael.

Chapter XI

Mr D G Malyon's Story

Our next short story comes from Mr D G Malyon, of Leicester. Mr. Maylon heard the War Time Memories programme that I did with that wonderful presenter for BBC Radio Leicester, John Florance. John is well known in Leicestershire, over the BBC air waves, for his Talkback programmes. It is always a privilege to be on air with John and to hear from his lovely listeners, when they share their War Time Memories with us. Thankfully Mr. Malyon, has forwarded his notes to me of his days in the Home Guard, during World War Two. I hope that you will find it of interest.

Home Guard 'Z Battery' LEI 101. A/A.

The first home guard unit that I joined was in 1942. It was mainly concerned with general defence training and I recall most sundays were spent defending people's back gardens. We were not very popular, so when the opportunity to be transferred to an Ack Ack unit arose for me, I did not hesitate for one moment. At that time most members of the home guard were men of the age group that were not likely to be called up ie, 45 to 50 year olds, or as in my case, lads of 16 to 17. The Ack Ack site that I was sent to was situated just on the outskirts of the city of Leicester, Victoria Park to be precise. During the day the site was manned by the Royal Artillery and on completing our training we took over at 8pm in the evening and finished at 7am in the morning. There were sufficient men recruited so that we were on duty every 8th night. Every sunday morning was spent on gun drill, which took in aircraft recognition, drilling and weapon instruction. The site was equipped with nine 'Z Battery' projectile firing Ack Ack guns and one bofors gun. Each gun was loaded with nine rockets, these were manually placed on rails. The shells weighed approximately 50lbs, they were six foot long and 3 inches in diameter. The firing taking place at quarter second intervals, through electrical contacts on the tail fin's. On the main platform of the gun were two cabins, one each side of the rails, in these cabins sat three of the gun crew. One of these would be the N.C.O. in charge of the gun, who also controlled the actual firing. The four shell loaders, sheltered in a brick emplacement at the rear, once the gun was loaded. The N.C.O. received orders through a headset, these orders coming from a command post, that were giving him bearings and trajectory instructions.

One of the many highlights while on this site was a railway trip to a firing camp at Heacham, on the Norfolk coast. Here we practiced firing Sten guns, better known as Tommy guns, into the sea. This really was rather tame compared to firing our rocket guns, at a 'Drogue' being towed by an aircraft, high up out over the sea. My enthusiasm in this task resulted in my promotion to Lance Corporal and I found myself in charge of a gun at the age of 16!

One incident that I will never forget happened one Sunday while at the firing camp. The drill was that when the process of firing had been completed the N.C.O. stepped out of the cabin on the gun platform, to check that all the projectiles had left the rails okay. On this occasion however, a solitary smoking shell still lay there. I had the gun placed in a safety bearing in case the projectile decided to fire and I reported a misfire to the command post. After waiting the five minutes, which was the standard time for misfires, I then had to order a loader to come and remove the offending round. I was not at all surprised when no one appeared and after waiting another five minutes I reported the situation to the command post. Almost immediately a Royal Artillery Sergeant, came forward. He lifted the rocket off the rails and marched off down the beach with it for approximately 100 yards, where he placed it on to a rack and calmly set about defusing it. A very brave man indeed.

The feature of this type of Ack Ack Battery was to create a box of exploding shells around an enemy aircraft. However based on experience during the London Blitz, the powers that be quickly discovered that the amount of shrapnel that was falling to the ground was creating more damage than the enemy bombs. As a result our bearing compasses were blanked out to avoid us firing over the city. It seemed the German pilots, were aware of this for they never approached the city on a bearing which allowed us to attack them. Consequently the guns on Victoria Park, were never fired in anger.

In 1944 we were stood down and shortly after, at the age of 17, I volunteered for the Army, which as they say would make another story. Thank you for allowing me to recall my memories of the Home Guard.

•

Dear Mr. Malyon,
Thank you for sharing some of your memories of World War Two with us. So many of us are aware of the TV comedy series and film of 'Dads Army' that we can well remember Corporal Jones and Private Pike and of course, their commanding officer Captain Mannering. We all laughed at the way they set about beating the enemy if they invaded our dear old England. I dare say there was much that you could relate to in the programme from your own days in the 'Home Guard'. Thank goodness that at your young age you were not like Private Pike, for I can see that you had great responsibility placed on your young shoulders. It has been a pleasure to write up your short story and to fly the flag in showing others of what we owe to you and your comrades, for the part you all played in giving us our today.
Yours most sincerely,
Michael Bentinck.

Chapter XII

Andrea Hoyland's Story

Those of you that have read my books 'War Time Women' and 'Waving Goodbye' will need no introduction to Andrea, as she has contributed some of her poems and of course that wonderful story featured in 'War Time Women' about her dear late mother who was a bus conductress (Clippee) and an A.R.P. in World War Two. Andrea first heard me many years ago now, on BBC Radio Lincolnshire, being interviewed by presenter Melvyn Prior. Andrea made contact with me and has been a great supporter n my work with my latest book, War Time Memories. When Andrea knew I was writing this book it wasn't long, thankfully, before she shared some more of her memories with me. I hope that you will enjoy reading this small piece of history.

Dear Michael,

I have sent you a few more memories of mine and one or two of the unpleasant things that my reticent husband told me about, of his part in World War Two. As I was writing about the different bombs which fell on Sheffield, I was reminded of a very recent incident which may amuse you, for by now I know that you are aware of my sense of humour. I recently had to buy a new gas cooker, as my old one was well past it's best. The new one was delivered and fitted by two workmen and when they were finished, I was instructed on all the dos and donts of how it worked. The younger man started telling me all about it and pointed out the starter button. I said "Oh yes, that of course works by battery?" He looked at me quite serious, "No, it's an automatic electronic ignition". He had no sense of humour and I could see that the other man was trying not to laugh. The younger man then pressed the button, turned on a tap and the ring lit up. When the button was pressed it made a ticking sound and he asked me if I knew what to do if it stopped ticking. Well after living through World War Two, I just could not resist the temptation, so I said "Yes, I run for my bloody life". The other man had to rush outside to laugh, while my instructor glared at me and said, "No dear, you'll want a new battery. I just hope that I don't look as stupid as he seemed to think I was.

Good luck with your new book and on behalf of all ladies, thank you for your generous donations to Breast Cancer Research. I send my very best wishes to you and Hilary and hope that you will enjoy the following memories.

In the past I have mentioned my late husband, Kenneth Hoyland, to you. He was only old enough to serve in the army from 1943. Like your dear late father and so many other brave men, no one could get him to speak very much about his experiences, although he went to Italy, Austria and Germany.

His regiment was the Royal Scots and they were some of the unfortunate young men to relieve the Belson concentration camp. Of the very few things he did tell me, was that on his arrival at the camp, the first thing he saw was a man who had sat on the ground and died, still cradling his dead friend in his arms. Kenneth had to help the shuffling souls, that had somehow managed to come out to greet their rescuers. Though most could hardly lift a bony arm, one poor man tried his best to stand at attention and salute, with tears pouring down his face. As you can imagine, my Kenneth was in tears as he recalled this story to me, for such memories never ever leave one. The worst thing for him must have been to stand among the stench and filth, while having his gun trained on captured Germans. These Germans had been ordered to dig the mass grave for the burial of the skeletal remains of some of the thousands who had been tortured and starved to death.

The weirdest thing happened a few years after Kenneth died at the young age of 54 years. I was watching a programme on television and saw some of the film that was taken at the time Belson was liberated. On a huge mound of earth stood a young British soldier, wearing the Royal Scots beret and as the camera moved around, I found myself looking at my dear late husband, as he stood guard above one of the mass graves.

I know that you have already featured my late mother, Doris Howard's, story of her experiences as an A.R.P. warden in your book 'War Time Women'. So now may I share with you my own war time memories, as an 8 year old in 1939. Also a poem which includes some of the thoughts a child would have way back then.

It is true to say, that I was shielded from the most awful things that war brings but by the time I had reached 14 years of age, I too had memories. Like sleeping under the heavy kitchen table, with all the furniture packed around it during an air raid, all because our anderson shelter was flooded. The siren suits my mother made, like an all in one boiler suit with hoods attached, which were made from thick army blankets. Although they were very warm they did make us itch all over. Our lovely garden, which was completely transformed into a large vegetable plot, with a hen house and chicken run, in our 'Dig for Victory' efforts. For a while when things were very bad and people were not allowed to gather in large groups, our school split the classes and we had lessons in the children's parent's homes. There were never more than 5 or 6 pupils attending at each house. Our teacher set the lessons at each of these and our hostess mother had to see that we did our work until the teacher returned. Consequently our school week was cut down by more than half. As older children talked among themselves, they became quite knowledgeable about things like the difference between incendiary bombs, molotov cocktails, land mines, time bombs, etc. Though they had been told not to, for obvious reasons, the boys went around the streets and gardens picking up spent shells and bomb shrapnel, so it's a wonder that more of them were not added to our casualty list.

When planes went overhead during the day, just by sight or the sound of it's engine most of us knew whether we should take shelter or not. Then one or another of us would shout "It's one of ours!".

On very rare occasions we witnessed dog fights over Sheffield, then later it would be re-enacted by crowds of mostly boys, zooming around and firing at a non-existent German plane, as none of them wanted to play the 'Gerry'.

As our dad worked on the air fields, he told us it was quite common for enemy planes to go off course and a couple of our fighters were scrambled quickly into the air to see them off.

After the blitz, mother took me into the town centre, to do some shopping, where I saw many of the grand old buildings and shops, which had become nothing more than a pile of rubble. She pointed out to me what had been a large hotel, in Fitzalan Square and told me a family friend had been killed while taking shelter in the cellar during a raid. I assure you, at times like those even a child can feel the horror of war. As always, mother was there to re-assure and tell me it would soon be over. So in 1945, it was finally over and I was 14 years of age and started my first job. Then it was a nine hour day, for five days a week, plus five hours on your half day. All this for £1.7s.6d a week, that's £1.37.

•

Dear Andrea,

Thank you once again for sharing some of yours and your loved ones War Time Memories, with us. So many of my readers that wrote to me after they had read 'War Time Women' mentioned your dear late mothers story. They told me of how they laughed, when they read how she was involved in the incident with the bus driver and the low bridge in Sheffield. I feel sure that she would be so proud of you, for thankfully as we can see she plays a big part in your War Time Memories. I must also say how I can imagine how your dear late husband, Kenneth, could never remove from his memory the sights that greeted him as he entered Belson.

As we have seen from some of the other stories, it is something that has stayed with so many people who found themselves trying to help those pour souls that suffered so much in Belson. As many have told me death was the only way to escape such inhuman suffering. If nothing else I really do hope that when young people read my books, they see to it that wars really are a thing of the past and that all nations can sort out their differences by getting round the table and discussing the problems to find a peaceful answer. I can hear many people reading this saying "He can dream" but surely if enough of us offer the hand of friendship, then one day mankind will learn before it really is to late for all of us. Take care Andrea and once again thank you.

Yours thankfully,

Michael

Chapter XIII

Edith Smith's Story

The following short story and poem come from Mrs Edith Smith of Rossendale, Lancashire. Mrs Smith, wrote to me to say how much she enjoyed the 'War Time Memories' programmes, that I have done over the last few years with BBC Radio Lancashire's presenters, Alison Brown and Jacquie Williams. In these programmes the good people of Lancashire have the chance to ring in and share their 'War Time Memories' with us and the listeners. Alison, Jaquie and I, are always touched by someone's moving story and equally happy to have a laugh when one of the listeners shares an amusing memory with us. I think it is very important to allow people that lived through World Wars, to share their memories in this way, if they wish to and I thank BBC Radio Lancashire so much for allowing me the privilege of hosting the programmes with such lovely presenters.

Dear Michael,
Thank you so much for allowing me to submit my short story and poems. I hope that you will find them of interest. Thank you for taking such an interest in the people that gave so much for our today and for your book 'Waving Goodbye' which I really did relate to as I read the wonderful true stories that evacuees, like me, had shared with you. I hope that you will find my poems of interest, and you have my permission to use them in your book, if you so wish.

I was evacuated twice in World War Two. The first time was soon after the Prime Minister, Neville Chamberlain's speech to the nation on 3rd September 1939. I don't think that anyone still alive today that heard this broadcast, will ever forget his words when he said, "I have to tell you now that this country is at war with Germany". It really was the start of six years of suffering and hardship for so many good folk.

I was soon evacuated from my home in Manchester, to Blackpool, at the tender age of 7 years old. I was one of the lucky ones and was billeted with a very kind family, who sadly lost a son in the early stages of the war, while I was staying with them. I remember that I saw my very first gold fish in Stanley Park and had my very first glimpse of the sea, all so very exciting for a seven year old. However I fretted so much for my parents that I had to be taken home.

Looking back I arrived home to face the blitz on Manchester and I remember seeing the bombs dropping. I later found out that some had dropped on Trafford Park. Many house's collapsed owing to the heavy bombing and we children would hunt for shrapnel, amongst the ruins.

The day soon came when we all had to marshall at school and I, like many other children, had only a pillow case with my clothes and a few possessions in. This was at London Street School, which later took a direct hit from the bombing. As we left that day we had our luggage labels tied to our coats and our little gas masks, in their boxes, slung over our shoulders. We marched off to the station, to be evacuated to Haslingden, where as you can see I have stayed ever since. When we arrived at Haslingden, the station was crowded with people who were consumed with curiosity as they watched us arrive. We walked all around the town with our teachers, who were begging people to take us in and give us a home. This we did for what seemed like hours and I know that even our teachers were exhausted. Eventually all but three children found homes to take them in. The three that were left, were a brother and sister and myself. I think our teacher, had given up hope of finding anywhere for us but, on seeing a lady in the road, our teacher approached her and asked if she would take us in. The lady at first said no, then she thought for a while and said, "I'll take the boy", she was told that he could not be parted from his sister. At this she stared at me then said, "I'll take her in. She looks like a little sparrow." I was taken in to her home and bathed and fed, then her own daughter was told to give up her bed for me to sleep in. She then had to sleep on a mattress, which was placed on a table, the mattress came from the W.R.V.S., I think that I was resented for this, as it was years later, that she forgave me and started to speak to me. My brother who had been evacuated with us had been separated from me and was billeted with a local councillor, who later became mayor. My brother searched for me for three months until he found me. He was only just over 9 years old but he never gave up trying to find me. Once he found me we would meet at his billet at the Councillor's house. We were told we could only use the back door but we were able to sit and talk in the kitchen together. So we decided that we would meet in the hills and play in the snow together. It was all very austere, oh how times have changed. Children, in the main, live in a much better world today. Eventually my parents arrived and they obtained a house in a village near by. We joined them and took up our lives together again, as families should. I still see the girl who was the last in our group to be billeted with her brother. Sadly her brother died a few years ago. All the things that happened to me then have, of course, become my War Time Memories. From my home today, I can look out of my window and see where I was billeted, known to many as a shop called Adams Stores. I, like many others that went to new places in the war, be it as Land Girls, Nurse's, Soldiers, Factory Workers, or even little evacuees, have stayed and made it my home for life.

•

Dear Edith,
May I be so informal and be on first name terms with you? Thank you for your kind words about the programme that I have the privilege to do now and again with your BBC Radio Lancashire. Thank you also for sharing with me a little of your memories of your days as that little evacuee in World War Two. It is my pleasure to feature your poems and I think the reader will see that they really do tell your story of that time in your life. May God bless and keep you safe.
Yours Most Sincerely,
Michael

The Evacuee
Edith M. Smith

The train was in the station,
At the onset of war.
A little girl sat quietly,
With tears not very far.
She wondered what was going on,
As folk ran up and down.
She entered a compartment.
Then the train steamed out of town.

She was on her way to Blackpool,
So very far from home.
Her parents she had left behind
Still in the danger zone.
She had her first glimpse of the sea,
And wondered what it was.
But it could never take the place
Of her dear mum and dad.

She loved them oh so dearly,
And wished that they were there,
To walk with her on golden sands,
And build castles in the air.
As time wore on the child did fret,
Her days were tinged with sadness.
With mum and dad so far away,
Yet she thought of them with gladness.

Eventually her dad did come,
and held her in his arms.
He said I've come to take you home,
I'll keep you safe from harm.
And with Gods grace the war will end,
And soon we'll be as one.
So dry your tears, dispel your fears.
Your lonely days are gone.

The Little Girl
Edith M. Smith

The little girl with head held high,
And tears all glistening in her eyes,
Clung tightly to her mothers hand,
As she walked across the pitted land.
A pillow case was all she had,
Inside her tiny clothes looked sad.
Her mother edged her to the station,
To join the others of the nation.

A hug a kiss as the train steamed in.
All aboard and out again.
A corner seat the child was weeping,
A glance around at others sleeping.
A sadness crept into her eye
As she thought of her mothers last goodbye.
At last the train stopped at a station,

With curious eyes and expectation.
The little girl stepped off the train,
Never to return again.
Snow lay thickly on the ground.
As the little children walked around.
No room for you was often spoken,
Unknown, unloved her heart was broken.
Until at last a voice was heard.
I'll take her in she's like a bird.
And so at last well warm and fed,
The little girl slept in a bed.

Time passed by until one day,
The little girl in church did pray.
God looked at her and he was moved,
Unknown to her his love was proved.
He answered her and sent her brother,
The two of them had found each other.
Locked together in warm embrace,
hand in hand the world they faced.
The little girl and now her brother,
Prayed silently they'd find their mother.
At last she came, Mother of pearl,
I know for I'm that little girl.

Chapter XIV

Anthony Dixon's Story

I end my stories section in this book with a story that shows how children of today are still learning of what life was like for people who had to live during the war. The following story comes from the son of my publishing editor, Keith Dixon. I had the privilege of being invited to Anthony's school to give my illustrated talk on 'Evacuees of World War Two'. Shortly afterwards the children went for the day to Stibbington, where they went back in time and became evacuees for a day. The following reflects, in Anthony's words, his memories and thoughts of that day.

I feel that it is very important that today's children learn of what it was like for children during World War Two, to understand the hardship and suffering that many dear little children had to endure at that time in their young lives.

I hope that all schools follow the direction that Anthony's school has, in showing children what life was like during this dreadful time. I am sure that it will teach the children a great deal but above all I hope that it will show them that war is not the way to solve any conflict. I hope they will learn that love and care for one another is the way to a better world.

For our history module at school, we were studying the war years 1939 to 1945. As part of this module we were looking at what life would have been like for the children who were evacuated from the big towns and cities, during World War Two. As part of this study my school, Bar Hill Primary, arranged for all year five children to visit the village of Stibbington, along the A1, near Peterborough. We were told that we would become evacuees for a day.

The week before we were due to go on the trip, we made gas mask boxes and labels to wear on our clothes. The labels had our name, age and school written on them. My teacher, Miss Hinchliffe, told us we had to imagine that we were children who were being evacuated from London. We looked at the sort of clothes that children wore during the war and we were told that on the morning of the trip we had to dress up in the same sort of clothes. We were all given names that were more common around 1939. I was given the name of George Graham, two of my class mates became my sisters and one became my brother. My sisters were given the names Rose and Ivy and my brother was called Arthur.

On the morning of our trip to Stibbington, I rushed out of bed and got dressed in my long shorts, white shirt, woollen jumper, long grey socks and black cap, which I had borrowed from one of my mum's friends. I put my gas mask box over my head and set off for school with my mum and sister, Paige. It was funny seeing all my friends walking to school dressed just like the boys and girls we had seen in the books a few days before.

We climbed on board the bus, outside the school and set off on our journey to Stibbington. It was strange seeing all my friends dressed as evacuees. As I waved goodbye to my mum and sister I did start to think about what it must have been like for those children 60 years ago, some of whom would have been younger than me, leaving home for real, not knowing when or if they would see their mums and dads again.

We soon arrived outside an old railway station in Stibbington. We all left the bus and went onto the station platform. It looked just as it would have done 60 years earlier. There were war-time posters on the walls and an old electric train stood on the tracks. We all climbed into one of the carriages and then two ladies, dressed in the way that ladies dressed in the 1940's, came in and introduced themselves and welcomed us to their village. Our day as true evacuees had started.

We were asked to describe the sort of things we saw on our journey, the sort of things which we wouldn't have seen as children during the war, living in London. Then one of ladies told us to line up and she inspected a few of us for nits. Then we had to show her our finger nails to make sure that there was no dirt under them.

After this inspection we left the train and went on a tour of the village. We eventually arrived at the village church and went inside. We were asked why we thought the bells were not ringing. I told the lady that it was because during the war the bells could only be rung as a warning that the Germans were invading. We then said a war-time prayer, asking God to protect all of the soldiers, then we sang a hymn.

After this small service we left the church and walked to the Stibbington Centre where we made an identity card to wear and then it was time for lunch. We were told that the sandwiches were filled with the sort of things that were available during the war: jam, cheese or spam. We were told that spam was an American meat sent over during the war. I didn't try the spam as it looked all thick with brown spots on. For desert we had spice cake and a drink of blackcurrant.

After lunch I exchanged my £1 coin for 2^1/$_2$p in old money which, although they were bigger coins, didn't sound like a lot of money. I bought a pad, pen, rubber, bookmark and two sweets from the shop. It was interesting to see what you could buy with just 2^1/$_2$p during the war. I packed the things that I had bought into my gas mask box and went outside to play war-time games in the playground with my friends. Some played with wooden guns, others played with hoola hoops, hoopla or hop scotch. It was fun but I did wonder what the children 60 years ago would make of the toys that my friends and I have to play with today.

After this break we went back inside and had a very interesting quiz about the war before moving into a classroom which was set out just as it would have been during the war. We sat on wooden chairs at wooden desks that had lids. Once everyone had found a desk and sat down, we were told to open the lids and take out the gas masks which were inside. We thought they were real ones but we were told they were replicas. We had to practice putting them on just in case the air raid siren went off during our lesson. The lady taking the class said that if she picked up the rattle and twisted it around making a noise, then that would be the signal that meant we had to rush to put our gas masks on. Later, during the spelling test, the teacher gave the signal and everyone rushed to get their gas masks out of the desk and on their heads. This all seemed very exciting but scary, at the time and I was glad that we were only pretending.

Once we had removed the gas masks and calmed down, we sat and listened to a recording of our Queen when she was a princess and evacuated during the war. Princess Elizabeth spoke to the boys and girls telling them that she knew how they were feeling, being away from their mothers and fathers, because she and her sister had now been evacuated to the country and were missing their parents.

Just as the Princess had finished we heard the noise of an aeroplane coming over. Then an air raid siren went off and we were led off excitedly to an air raid shelter. We stood around inside the shelter singing songs that children sang during the war. We sang 'Run Rabbit Run', 'Run Hitler Run' and 'It's a long way to Tipperary'.

When we came out of the air raid shelter, we were told that our guardians were ready to take us to their house's, which turned out to be our teachers ready to take us back to school.

We had a very interesting and exciting day at Stibbington. We definitely got a feel of what life was like for evacuated children during the war. I was glad I was a schoolboy now and not during the war. I realise how much more I have to play with and how much better I eat, than children 60 years ago. It must have been a frightening and sad time for the children.

•

Dear Anthony,

Thank you for sharing with us your time as a little evacuee. I know that you have read my book of true stories all about evacuees called 'Waving Goodbye' but, having seen the pictures of you in your evacuee clothes, I know that you are aware of how lucky you are that you only had to wear them for one day. As you now know the little evacuees of World War Two usually had only one set of clothes to wear and many of them would have bits of cardboard in their shoes to cover the holes in the soles. Today such people know just how lucky they are to have the things that they have today and after their hardships as children, they appreciate all they have. Always remember Anthony that these people have worked hard to give us the wonderful things that we take for granted today and they can be so proud to say 'Oh I was one of those little evacuees'. You work hard and learn all that you can at school for, believe it or not, these really are some of the best times in your life.

God bless you,

Michael

Letters & Poems

Letter from Mrs. M. Rose. Folksworth, Peterborough.

Dear Mr Bentinck,

It was so nice to speak with you on the phone yesterday, following your guest spot on Mandy Morton's programme for BBC Radio Cambridgeshire. I always enjoy the War Time Memories programmes that you and Mandy do together as they evoke so many memories for me. Please do make allowances for my writing as I have bad arthritis now in my hands and joints.

My worst recollection of World War Two and I imagine for thousands of others, is one that I have not heard mentioned, or read about, in war time books. Perhaps it was the great feeling of relief when the war finished that obliterated it from people's minds. It wasn't the sound of German planes overhead, or the heavy bombing raids. It wasn't the blackouts, rationing, or all the other shortages that we had to put up with, because we coped with all of those. It was the sight of the telegraph boy coming down the lane that was the worst sight anyone could hope to see. As he slowly cycled along, you prayed that he was not heading towards your house. There would be such a feeling of relief when he passed your house. This relief was soon replaced with sadness though, as you knew that he would be going to one of your neighbours, who of course we would know. We would hope against hope that he would not be delivering the worst news to them. We didn't have to wonder where he had been for long, for in those days, even though our lane was a long one, everyone knew everyone else. Sadly so many dear boys that we knew were lost in the war but thankfully my two brothers, who served throughout the war, returned home safely to make our family whole again. Alas for so many others it was not to be and as you say Michael, it really is the everyday ordinary families, that really

140

do suffer in wars. Like you, I hope and pray that mankind will learn before it really is too late for us all.
Best Wishes,
Mary Rose.

Dear Mary,

Thank you for your letter and for your kind words about the programme that Mandy and I are privileged to do for the listeners. As you know it really is the listeners that make the programmes so good, as they share their memories with us over the airwaves. I know, like you, that so many dear families received those hurtful telegrams, my own dear grandparents received one saying that my father was missing in action, believed killed. Thankfully the powers that be were wrong and my dad had only been captured and went on to survive the nightmare of hell on earth and returned home after the war. As you so rightfully say, for so many dear people it was not to be and it is to those dear brave souls that we owe our today. Thank you for sharing your memory of those fateful days with us.

Kind Regards,
Michael

•

Letter from Mr Alvan A Eames, Blackburn, Lancashire

I have enjoyed your War Time Memories programmes that you do with our Jacquie Williams and Alison Brown, on our BBC Radio Lancashire. I thought you might like to read a little of my war time memories from World War Two, with my grandparents. Such memories are priceless.

I was born at Cleethorpes, in the village of Nettleton. We lived in a small cottage with one cold tap, called a faucet, for water. We had no electricity or gas and the privy was down at the bottom of the garden.

We moved across Lancashire five years later but my brother and I were sent back to Nettleton when the war broke out in 1939, to live with our grandma and grandpa in their cottage.

We had a battery driven wireless set which had a 90 volt HT battery and the low tension was looked after by glass accumulators, of which we had two. One in the wireless set and one at the local garage, being recharged.

One day Grandpa told us that there had been a report on the wireless that there was to be a German air raid that night and we had better dig a trench in the garden in which to take shelter. My young brother, Pat and I dug a trench about 4 feet by 3 feet and 4 feet deep. We included a step at one end to facilitate Grandma's descent. The trench was amongst the redcurrant and blackcurrant bushes.

We were not allowed to stay up for the air raid but were sent to bed as usual, by candle light, with the promise that we would be woken up in good time for the air raid.

Of course we slept right through until morning with no air raid, much to our disappointment and found, to out utter astonishment, that the trench had vanished and the lavatory had been emptied - there was a good fruit crop that year!

Best wishes
Alvan Eames

•

Letter from Rosalie Martin
I received this wonderful letter from Rosalie Martin, it's about her war time experiences in the A.R.P and Civil Defence during the war.

Just before the outbreak of the Second World War, several of us in the Girl Guides were asked to join the A.R.P. and civil defence. I was 16 years old at the time and our job was to man the telephones in the village hall, which was joined to the Hawkinge airfield. I lived next door to the Village Hall with my parents and brother. I also had the first aid kit, as I had been a St John's first aider as a Guide.

We were at our post when war was declared and the gas masks had to be taken out to the villagers immediately. As I knew the countryside well I was asked to go with a car driver to deliver them. It was midday and I remember going to tell my parents what I was going to do, my father did not approve, I can remember him saying 'Your mother is just dishing up the Sunday dinner', never the less I went and we got them all delivered. Before we could start to deliver these gas masks we had to go to Lyminge to have our identity cards stamped so that we could cut across the airfield should we need to at anytime.

Then one night when all the German bombers were coming over the airfield, on their way to London, the siren went off and I jumped out of bed to take a look out of my bedroom window. My attention was caught by someone from a house at the top of the airdrome road flashing a light, as if to signal to the planes. I happened to notice this on three nights running. I told my parents, who informed the Sergeant of the buffs that they knew and he came and questioned me. The next time there was an air raid the house was watched and the same thing happened again and as it turned out a SPY was caught.

The aerodrome was always a target, so we spent many nights in our air raid shelter, which at the beginning of the war was across the road and a little way up in the vicarage grounds. Once, when I was crossing the road a bomber came straight over my head and dropped a bomb on the shelter just in front of me, killing all the occupants, all of whom I knew very well. The men of the A.R.P. wouldn't let us girls go to help, so I handed over the first aid kit but it wasn't needed, it was a direct hit and there were no survivors. The men dug out the remains, which were then taken to the village hall. We were eventually given a Morrison Shelter, which was put in our sitting room.

On the 16th January 1942, at the age of eighteen years and four months, I joined the A.T.S Voluntary Service. I went to the Guildford training centre and my Army number was W/122683 Pte. R.A. Gardner. My brother was in the Home Guard and my father was called upon to do airfield maintenance which, with the help of many more men, was to keep filling in the bomb craters on the runways.

On the 11th February, I was posted to 520 battery, Anzac Barracks, Devizes, Wiltshire, for signal and telephonist training. On 10th March I was posted to 6th Heavy Ack Ack Practice camp, Cleeve, Bude, North Cornwall. I enjoyed it there as it was only March and yet it was summer weather. I went on leave from there and I had a lovely suntan when I arrived at Folkestone railway station which was covered in thick snow.

I was then stationed mainly in the Hull area, at one of our places. Our base was in the outskirts of Hull and we had to be taken by truck to our gunsite. I remember once when it was thick snow, the trucks couldn't get on the road, so our officer went to the farm up the road and borrowed the farmers horse and sleigh to carry our rations, we had to walk behind. The farmer stopped at his farm on the way as his wife had cocoa and cake for us, we sat on bales of straw eating and drinking before setting off again in the snow.

The command post and all of our sleeping accommodation was under canvas and in the snow it was very cold. While I was on duty one night one of our spotters came to me and said "One of the Mongolian prisoners of war has told me that the radio MUST GO!" I eventually stopped laughing and got her to understand that he wanted the Radio Moscow programme which, of course, he didn't get.

On 6th May 1943 I was with 519 (M) H.A.A. Battery at Creswick Green Camp, Ecclesfield, Sheffield, as a telephonist. One day all the camp were confined to barracks, owing to somebody doing something wrong. Our hut was slightly away from the rest and as it was mine and a couple of other girl's half day off we decided that as time off was hard to come by, we couldn't waste it sitting in the hut, so we got dressed and crept out and around the back of the hut. The other girls in our barrack room lifted the wire fencing so that we could slide underneath. When we came back later that night they helped us get back in the same way. We were never missed.

On June 8th 1943 I was still with 519 battery. We were now stationed at Whitby practice camp. On one of our route marches I recall that on one occasion our Officer took us on a march to the local Abbey. We had to climb the 144 steps, or more, to the Abbey and we sat on Draculars tombstone. The Officer had brought sweets along and handed them out. We had a lovely day although some came back with blisters but I was lucky.

I was posted to 524 battery on 9th January 1944, H.A.A. R.A. and we were around the Hull area until 25th August 1945. We spent most of that time at Long Lane Camp, Preston, on the Costello playing fields. We used to go to Spurn Point, which was a lovely place to visit when off duty, we used to go along the sand dunes. There was a big ship anchored off Spurn Point and one of our officers went out to it and came back with a lot of fish. So we had fried, fresh fish for tea. Also at Spurn Point my friend, Rose Stakes and I went out in a rowing boat with a crew. This was our first attempt at rowing.

There was to be a big parade on the camp at Costello playing fields, the corporal made us telephonists and spotters go on parade, even though we had just come off night duty. I think there were about 8 of us, so we arranged beforehand that when the sergeant gave an order "Right turn quick march", we would do a left turn and march in the opposite direction. This we did and the sergeant yelled "Haaalt" at the top of his voice. He then shouted "Telephonists and Spotters about turn, quick march", when we joined the rest of the parade he shouted "Telephonists and Spotters fall out and never come on parade again", so we won!

These are just some of the little things that we got up to during those dreadful years during the war. I was later transferred to the Royal Army Medical Core on 10th November 1945 and finished up at A.T.S., C.R.S. Woodlands, Kaffir Road, Huddersfield, until I was demobbed on 1st. April 1954.

•

Letter from Mr R H Jamieson, Mildenhall, Suffolk

Dear Mr Bentinck,

I have recently read your book War Time Women and found it very enjoyable. In it I note that you say you might write another on similar lines, consequently I am enclosing my recollections of February 1941, in case it may be of some use to you.

Shortly after the outbreak of World War Two, I joined, the then, ARP as a Messenger. I was also a pupil at Newmarket Grammar School, now Foley House.

On 18th February 1941, a Market day, whilst in class, I well remember the Air Raid siren sounding, as the rest of the school took shelter underneath the metal staircase, I collected my cycle and rode to the Report Centre at Newmarket Tech, now Fen Fones. I hadn't been there very long when we heard an aircraft approaching and then explosions. A number of us went into the woodwork room at the back of the building, from there we could see clouds of smoke and immediately thought the Grammar School had been hit. Luckily we were to learn later that it hadn't. However we very soon learnt that the High Street had been very seriously damaged and that there were a large number of casualties. At the same time we found that all the telephones were not working, owing to the Post Office and Telephone Exchange having been hit by one of the bombs.

Later that evening we were informed that emergency telephones lines had been established from the 'outside world' to Kentford and to the Doric Cinema, now De Niros and that we messengers were required to man the Doric Cinema, which we did for the next three days and nights until proper telephone links were established.

That first night I was required to deliver a message to the temporary mortuary situated in Old Station Road and can still, after all these years, remember the bodies laid out in the room.

The following night there was an Alert and we messengers were required to go around the different points at which there were Air Raid Sirens and notify the persons in charge to sound them. My order was to go to the ARP Warden's base at the New Wellington public house in Cheveley Road, where the siren was attached to a very large pole. Later in the early hours of the morning the 'All Clear' came through and we were required to go round again and get the 'All Clear' sounded. Luckily the third night was Alert free and we were able to get some rest.

During these three days and nights we were on duty at the Doric, only going home for meals. The operations base was in the foyer of the Cinema and we tried to rest and sleep on the large sofa type seats. The Cinema remained opened for business after the first night.

On the fourth day telephone connections were established and we were no longer required to be on duty. A couple of nights later I was on duty again at the Report Centre. Strangely, within a week we were all issued with tin hats!

I well remember those tragic and traumatic days but looking back, I suppose they were rather adventurous ones for a fourteen year old.

Roy Jamieson.

On Behalf Of All Senior Citizens
Andrea Hoyland.

A huge Millennium Dome, oh dear! What have you done?
Well it looks so ridiculous, we're bound to poke some fun.
Was it built to match your ego, for that must be quite large,
And will you get your money back, by heck! You'll have to charge.
Or did you want it seen from way up there in space,
So aliens will bring their ships to park within the place.
Then there are the refugees who have no clothes or home.
It would make good sense if they could come and live inside the dome.
Each time there is some great event, someone starts to build,
I suppose they'll go on doing it till all our land is filled.
We have wonderful Cathedrals to celebrate our Lord,
Palaces were built for those who could afford,
Prince Albert's Crystal Palace, made entirely of glass,
But you must admit they all had style, great flair and class.
At the Festival of Britain we acquired a concert hall,
Another useful building, though in comparison quite small.
Big is not so beautiful if tornados come our way,
Let's face it, one great effort and it could blow away.
If your Millennium Dome is there for all to see,
Then what about the poor folk who can't afford the fee?
What's done is done, you finished the mammoth task.
We preferred a Millennium Grant - but then you never asked.

A young Girls War
Andrea Hoyland

Sat upon my windowsill, when I should have been asleep.
I looked out at the garden so colourful and neat.
The rockery with shades of green and flowers oh so white,
Which seemed to nod in the evening sunshine bright.
The huge tree at the bottom which I loved to climb
But big brother used to tell on me, every single time.
The fresh green lawn below me as I sat.
The moths that were tormented by our crazy cat.
Over on the other side our rabbit's little homes,
Two beautiful Angora's we had to brush and comb.
Mum and Dad's quiet voices drifting up to me,
As they sat out in the garden drinking cups of tea.
Then I slept upon the sill till mother came to check.
"One day she'll fall and break her blooming neck".

Eleven O'clock one morning we sat without a noise.
Our parents were so solemn as they listened to the voice.
Then everything was changing in my perfect little land.
First my father went away and I didn't understand.
Mum went into her garden and dug the biggest hole.
When I asked big brother he said, "She's looking for a mole".
We went out to help and I held the bolts and spanner,
But this job wasn't going right and I'm sure mum said "Oh damn her".
Our air raid shelter finally up, she then made siren suits.
In the garden once again she picked off all the fruits,
Pulled out all the bushes and dug from end to end.
Planted veg and tatters on which we must depend.
The chickens all arrived and housed within a run,
Now they really pleased me, with them I'd have such fun.
The first time sirens woke us, we rushed out to take our place
In the Anderson shelter, where we would all be safe.
Opening the door we found to our dismay,
The thing was full of water, so we ran the other way.
Had mother dug so deep that she had tapped into a well.
So it had to be re-sighted and then you couldn't tell.

Our Dad had joined the Air Force but kept his feet upon the ground,
He serviced British bombers and mended holes he found.
We had the Sheffield Blitz which terrified us all
But the British bulldog in us, meant we weren't about to bawl.
Those without a home came to live with those who had.
We tried to laugh about it, although it was so sad.
Two soldiers came to stay awhile, from Dunkirk we were told.
It was years before I realised why they shivered so with cold.
Gone six years of our lives and Dad was home at last,
In his grey demob suit, with trousers at half mast.
Didn't have his size but I don't think he cared,
As long as he could buy a pint and they would pay his fare.

The A.R.P. disbanded so mum hung up her hat.
Our family sat together and Dad said, "Well that's that".
So I sat upon my windowsill and gazed out at my tree,
And thanked God that my family were all home and free.
Then I looked into the garden and saw that 'Thing' out there,
Now a mass of runner beans but mother wouldn't care.
She was bound to have us digging till the Anderson was gone.
Sunday we had chicken, "Where's the cockerel Mum?".
We all need a holiday but will have to wait and see.
One thing is for certain, this "young lady" won't be climbing trees.

I leave you readers with this poem by Sydney Dinsdale who was in the East Yorkshire Regiment. It sums up all the reasons why we should and must, stop on the 11th November each year to remember those that gave up their lives so that you and I and our children, can have our today in peace.

Their sacrifice be undimmed by space or time, nor pride in them debased in later years, by unremembering and selfishness. That we, in truly honouring those who gave, leave to our heirs just cause to honour us.

Remembering
Sydney Dinsdale

Remembrance Day, we turn a page back to those gone,
They do not age like we, their dear ones,
family, kin and comrades -
welded in the din of War,
who mourn, not just Remembrance Day.

Young then they were and strong and tall,
and others - not so young but all gave what they had,
their strength, their skill, their lives,
and memory stirs us still
to mourn them this Remembrance Day

We meet once more, though aren't here
who spoke and clasped our hands last year,
They too will stay on in the mind
of those they loved, now left behind
to mourn them, this Remembrance Day

Is it enough then that we rise
recalling them in our minds eyes
just once each year?
save but the few who miss them, every day anew,
more deeply, each Remembrance Day.

Their children, what inherit they
a failing Britain? Tired and grey?
Dear Lord forbid; where is our pride in nationhood?
for which they died,
look round you this Remembrance Day.

This 'Band of Brothers' happy breed
our great Bard named us, now we need again,
their will to win - their zeal
for Britain's sake, it wounds to heal,
take heart on this Remembrance Day

Let's make this land a better place,
for all, unheeding creed or race,
share what we have, we did before,
and won - an awful, bloody war
what say you? this Remembrance Day

End Note

Well my friends, once again we have come to the end of our journey through another of my books. I hope that you have enjoyed your trip and have found all the stories of great interest. Every time I write one of these true stories, I myself learn more about the everyday people that gave so much for our today. It enforces in me my belief that we must never, ever, forget the importance of the 11th November 'Remembrance day' - when we can take time to reflect on what so many good people gave for us to have a life today.

I always enjoy doing my one man 'War Time Memories' shows for the Royal British Legion, around our country, for I know that it is helping to raise funds for the good work that they do in caring for our dear war heroes. As those of us who have not lived through the nightmare of a world war grow older, it is us that must teach the younger ones of the sacrifice that so many people gave for us to live in peace. So many of us look around our world today and say "Whatever would those good people, who laid down their lives for us in the war, think if they could see the state our world is in today". Well let's all work that bit harder to offer the hand of friendship to all God's children, whatever colour or creed they may be. Then perhaps we can all live in peace together and make the sacrifice that so many made, seem worthwhile.

Wear your poppies with pride my friends as you remember them.

•

If you would like information about my books on audio cassette, please do visit my website: www.michaelbentinck.com
or write to: Bentinck Books, 10 Henry Morris Road, Impington, Cambridge, CB4 9YG.